DIVORCE IN POLAND

STUDIES IN THE SOCIAL SCIENCES

edited by C. A. O. van Nieuwenhuijze

5

DIVORCE IN POLAND

A CONTRIBUTION TO THE SOCIOLOGY OF LAW

by

JAN GÓRECKI

1970

MOUTON

THE HAGUE · PARIS

LIBRARY OF CONGRESS CATALOG CARD NUMBER: 77 - 102956

Printed in The Netherlands by Mouton & Co., Printers, The Hague.

ACKNOWLEDGMENTS

I would like to take the opportunity of thanking all those who helped me in collecting the empirical data utilized in this study. These are, in particular, the persons interviewed: 41 judges and 60 barristers of Cracow, Warsaw, Lublin and Katowice, 152 divorced and reconciled persons, 323 evening students of law at the University of Cracow. I wish to express my thanks to the authorities and judges of the County Court in Cracow for enabling me to attend the divorce trials and for access to court records; to the Statistical Department of the Ministry of Justice for access to unpublished statistical data; to the Address Office of the City Council in Cracow for information about addresses of persons to be interviewed. Next, my thanks go to the Public Opinion Research Centre in Warsaw for arranging, at my request, a survey covering the whole country. I am especially indebted to Mrs. T. Dobrowolska, University of Cracow, and Mrs. A. Zambrzycka-Kunachowicz, the Academy of Sciences, for obtaining interviews with divorced and reconciled persons, and to Dr. J. Steczkowski, Cracow School of Economics, for his comments on the statistical aspect of the study. I am also grateful for the support of the Department of Civil Law, University of Cracow, which enabled me to pay for interviews with divorced and reconciled persons, and to arrange journeys to collect factual data from the districts of the courts in Warsaw, Lublin and Katowice. My warm thanks go to Miss Miriam Gallaher of the Center for Advanced Study in the Behavioral Sciences, Stanford, for correcting the proofs and making the last minute linguistic amendments while I was a Fellow at the Center.

CONTENTS

I

THE METHOD AND SUBJECT OF THE STUDY

1.1. The method applied in this study differs from that commonly in use in the legal sciences; the study is based on empirical investigations. My intention was not to analyse the meaning of the legal provisions (though a brief description of them cannot be omitted), but to find out how they work, i.e. to bring to light whether, in what degree and in what way their aims are being achieved. Hence — the explanation of these aims and the empirical investigation of their attainment constitute the main contents of the study.

Not all legal institutions may form the topic of this type of study. Only provisions in frequent use, the working of which can be observed on broad factual data, are suitable; and provisions the effects of which are controversial: for, if they were obvious, bringing them to light would be a discovery of mere commonplace facts.

The provisions concerning divorce meet both the above requirements. Divorce is a frequent phenomenon: its frequency, during the decade 1955–1964, is shown in Table 1. Moreover, the effects of these provisions are a controversial issue not only in Poland, but in all the countries which accept divorce. Hence the choice of the topic indicated in the title of the present study. It should, however, be pointed out that the title is not entirely accurate; not all the functional problems connected with divorce will be fully presented below. The main consideration will concern the provisions on breakdown of marriage as ground for divorce. To the working of the other norms, in particular those concerning the effects of divorce and the child's situation in the divorce suit, less attention will be paid than they would deserve in a detailed report on divorce problems as a whole. Nevertheless, they will, because of their close connection with the question of breakdown, be presented within such limits that the use of the word "divorce" in the title of the study, and not only of the expression "breakdown of marriage", seems to be justified.

TABLE 1

*Number of Final Divorce Decrees *) Pronounced and Divorce Rate in Poland: 1955–1964*

Year	Number of final divorce decrees pronounced	Final divorce decrees per 10,000 of the total population
1955	13,294	4.9
1956	13,816	5.0
1957	15,681	5.5
1958	15,704	5.5
1959	15,422	5.3
1960	14,882	5.0
1961	16,407	5.5
1962	17,954	6.0
1963	19,455	6.3
1964	20,938	6.7

*) On decrees "final" see below, p. 16, footnote 4.

1.2. Thus the purposes of the provisions on breakdown of marriage and their fulfilment will be the main subject of the further considerations. The expression "purpose of legal provision" is far from being unambiguous. Here it denotes those effects which, according to the intention of its makers, the provision is intended to produce: the legal norms are here considered as tools used consciously by the legislator to achieve aims.

Obviously, not all these aims can be ascertained with full clarity. To put the matter more broadly: precise ascertainment of the aims intended by the makers of any legal institution seems to be hardly possible. For, firstly, these makers are usually an entity not easily to be defined. Secondly, their views on the subject under regulation are often controversial. Moreover, each of them can for mixed reasons influence the content of the provision to be enforced. These are, *inter alia*, the difficulties which have made the problem of the so-called "legislator's will" a traditionally controversial issue in jurisprudence. Despite these difficulties, however, some fundamental purposes of the divorce provisions, as of many other legal institutions, can be defined with sufficient precision for the needs of a study treating the norms in a functional manner. There are certain indications which make this possible. The first of them is, sometimes, the very content of a given provision, when explained against its social and historic background. The second – various historic data connected with its enactment, in particular discussions preceding the enactment, as well as the motives published by the legislative bodies or their members. Another, supplementary indication is the decisions of the Supreme Court: they frequently explain why a given norm has been issued.

Let me mention now, in anticipation, those purposes of the Polish divorce provisions which will be analysed below in greater detail. There are three fundamental goals. The first is to assure a liberal, but not too liberal access to divorce: if a marriage has become a failure, let the spouses be free to dissolve their union only when the breakdown of their marriage is indeed complete and permanent. The second aim is that the court should overcome conflicts between the spouses and bring about a reconciliation whenever possible. Lastly, there are some moral and pedagogical goals of the rule of recrimination which prevents, in principle, the solely guilty spouse from claiming divorce. These three purposes determine the structure of the present study; the subsequent parts will deal with breakdown of marriage, reconciliation and recrimination.

II

COLLECTING EMPIRICAL DATA

2.1. To learn whether, to what extent and in what way these three purposes are being realised, it was necessary to collect a great deal of factual data throwing light on the whole course of divorce trial, on some antecedences and behind-the-scenes happenings of the trial, and on some elements of the situation which emerges after divorce. I initially intended to start by studying a sample of the court records. Nevertheless, the idea has been rejected, since there appears evident discrepancy between the contents of the court records and the factual course of the divorce suit. This discrepancy occurs as early as at the conciliatory session: only the outcome of the session – usually the fact that "the attempt to bring about a reconciliation of the parties gave no result" – is recorded, not its course. That is why in all those instances where the conciliatory activity of the court is not limited merely to putting a formal question as to the possibility of reconciliation, the discrepancy between the actual course of the session and contents of records is considerable; and the more intense the conciliatory activity, the larger is this discrepancy. On the other hand, the discrepancy between the further course of the trial and contents of the court records varies, depending on the conscientiousness of the judge. However, even with the most scrupulous judges, the record is but an abbreviation of events that occur in the courtroom. For, only those declarations of the parties and other participants of the suit which are of import in deciding the case are recorded. Moreover, not only the words used are an important element of the parties' behaviour. There are also their moods, emotional stresses, various personality traits which come out in the courtroom, but are not reflected in the court records. Moreover, in the courtroom the judge, laymen and barristers take part in the drama of the divorce suit not only by speaking, but also by their gesture and facial expression; in the court records only their words come out. Obviously, one should not exaggerate, and deny the value of the records as a source of information. Nevertheless, their value is certainly limited and merely supplementary, and only direct observation may be used as a basic source of information. That is why an observation of conciliatory sessions and of the further course of divorce suits appeared necessary.

2.2. I attended the divorce suits in the County Court of Cracow, which embraced a population of approximately 2,022,700 persons, of which 495,600 were inhabitants of Cracow and 1,527,100 inhabitants of the province. During the period of my investigations there were 6 divorce judges in the Cracow Court. The observation of trials, preceded by a pilot study, started at October 1, 1961, and continued till June 30, 1963. The sample consisted of 153 trials. I chose them at random, entering in turn the courtrooms where divorce cases were being tried by various judges and spending a couple of days in each room till the moment when observation of 153 trials started; then I continued attending the adjourned cases. The number of cases taken from each judge was proportional to his caseload. Each case was attended from the stage in which I found it when entering the courtroom; but I did not start attending those cases which were so advanced that at least one of the parties had already been heard by the court; for, the parties' testimony was of particular import in my inquiry. Proceeding in this way I attended 123 trials from the first sitting (but not from the conciliatory session), 20 – from the second, 6 – from the third, 4 – from the fourth. Each trial was attended till the decree of the first instance, provided that the decree was pronounced, which was the case in 140 suits. If there was an appeal (which happened in 12 cases), I reconstructed the course of the appeal proceedings from the court records, treated here as a supplementary source of information. I also reconstructed from the court records the course of the sittings preceding the beginning of my observation.

To calculate what the proportion of this sample to the whole population was, I have taken as a base of the calculation the total number of decrees of the first instance pronounced in the divorce cases in Cracow in the period from October 1, 1961 till June 30, 1963. There were 2621 decrees, *i.e.*, those pronounced in the suits attended amounted to 5.3 per cent. There appeared, however, in the course of the observation, some difficulties which had a negative impact on the contingency of the sample. First, there were 3 cases in which I was asked to leave the courtroom: according to an agreement with the court authorities I was allowed, because of the principle of closed doors in divorce suits, to attend the sittings provided that neither party objected. Moreover,

I was unable, because of collisions between adjourned sittings and of other time factors to attend 19 cases till the decree, through all the adjournments, which were therefore superseded by other cases additionally drawn. It was a drawback resulting from the fact that I attended all the trials personally; on the other hand, that I was unassisted resulted in a fully homogenous evaluation of the collected factual data.

It can be seen from what has been said above that my observation was not limited to 153 trials: fearing to lose some of them, I began, after having started the observation of 153, to attend a certain number of cases as a reserve. 19 of them substituted for those lost. There remained a surplus, in which I also included some further suits, in particular the 19 that dropped out: they fell out of the main sample, but were partially attended. The total surplus was composed of 34 cases which will be utilized below as a supplementary source of examples, and not as a basis for generalizations.

2.3. The observation of conciliatory sessions was simpler. I did not observe the sessions in the above mentioned suits attended, because attending of the suits from the conciliatory session would have resulted in too great a prolongation of the time and scope of the inquiry; that is why the sample of conciliatory sessions was drawn from the other trials. The sample was composed of 84 sessions taken from each judge at random, in proportion to his caseload. I attended the sessions in the period from October 1, 1961 till June 30, 1962. Since during that period 1,240 conciliatory sessions were conducted altogether in the Cracow Court, the sample amounted to 6.8 per cent. I was asked twice to leave the courtroom, which diminished the contingency of the sample.

When attending the conciliatory sessions and the further course of divorce trials, I did not inform anybody, and in particular not the judges, of the purpose of my inquiry: if they had known that their behaviour was, *inter alia,* the subject of observation, they probably would not have behaved as usual. The judges, as well as barristers with whom I came in touch in the courtroom, thought that I was recording the causes of breakdown: they frequently made this belief known, advising me to become acquainted with such and such a case where the causes were, in their opinion, interesting. Neither did my presence influence the attitude of the parties. Only in exceptional cases did the parties ask what I was doing in the courtroom: they usually thought I was a barrister waiting for the next case or, not being well acquainted with court proceedings, believed I was another participant in the suit.

2.4. The data collected this way reflect a fragment of Cracow Court practice. To gather more information from the courtroom I drew on the experience of others, and interviewed, in 1963, the judges and barristers of Cracow as well as of some other parts of Poland: Warsaw, Lublin and Katowice. I was unable to arrange interviews in all the 44 divorce courts in Poland. I chose the ones mentioned because they differ in some degree from each other as to population and legal training, i.e. those two factors which influence the course of a divorce suit to a large extent; therefore it seemed that if considerable divergencies existed in the practice of various Polish courts, they would probably come to light in the interviews from these four courts. On the other hand, if similarities appeared between these four courts, they would probably be characteristic of the majority, if not of all the divorce courts in Poland.

In order to draw on the experience of judges, I intended to interview all the divorce judges of Warsaw, Cracow, Lublin and Katowice. There were altogether, at the time of my inquiry, 43 judges: 26 in Warsaw, 7 in Lublin, 6 in Cracow and 4 in Katowice [1]. Since 2 of them, because of prolonged illness, were absent from court, I succeeded in 41 cases. At the beginning of the interview I asked each judge about the approximate number of divorce trials and conciliatory sessions conducted by him during his judicial career. All the judges interviewed had together been charged with the conducting of more or less 26,750 divorce trials, and approximately 25,700 conciliatory sessions; the difference between these two figures results from the fact that the court sometimes omits the conciliatory session [2].

The number of barristers in all the above mentioned courts is so great, that I had to limit myself to interviews with a very small part of them. There were two ways of doing this: either to draw a representative sample or to interview only those barristers who knew me fairly well or to whom I had been introduced by a person they trusted. I chose the latter way: some of the questions which I had to ask them aimed at obtaining rather confidential information on the manner of

[1] The number of the judges, in the courts of Cracow and Katowice, is not so large, because in those courts divorce judges conduct divorce suits only. This is not the case in Warsaw and Lublin, where each judge combines the trial of various kinds of suits. That is why in Lublin, where the number of the divorce cases is smaller, divorce judges are more numerous than in Cracow and Katowice. On the other hand in Warsaw, where divorce judges also conduct other kinds of suits, and the number of the divorce cases is large, the number of judges is highest.

[2] See on this below, p. 23.

conducting divorce suits, and I therefore preferred to be assured of their sincerity rather than of the representativeness of the sample. They seemed to be sincere, sometimes to the extent of spontaneously telling me about abuses they themselves had committed, in particular of the way which they had deceived the court. I got 60 interviews: 25 with barristers from Cracow, 15 from Warsaw, 10 from Lublin and 10 from Katowice. I asked each barrister how many trials he had taken part in since July 1958, i.e. when divorce suits had been transferred to the competence of the county courts [3]. They represented altogether experience drawn from more or less 4280 divorce trials and 4235 conciliatory sessions.

2.5. The above enquiries did not furnish all the information needed. It appeared that it was necessary to learn something of the behind-the-scene elements of divorce trials, as well as some of their antecedences and sequences. Hence – interviewing of divorced persons and of those reconciled in the course of the trial.

The main sample of divorcees has been completed on the basis of records of the Cracow County Court. I drew the sample from the first 488 suits which had been brought during the period between January 1 and April 13, 1959. It seemed justifiable to choose this period since the county courts started to conduct divorce suits on July 12, 1959. I intended to draw the sample from the suits which had started as early as possible, because the earlier their introduction, the higher the proportion of those finally concluded. Nevertheless, I did not take the sample from the second half of 1958: it seemed that in the initial period a court's practice is never quite normal, and that it takes at least some months to get it into its normal stride.

The majority of those 488 cases did fall out, a considerable number of them because of the territorial limitation of the examined population: interviews were conducted only in cases where the court records indicated that at least one of the spouses lived in Cracow. Some other cases were not concluded until the end of collecting empirical data or resulted in dismissal, discontinuation or suspension of proceedings, or return of petition because the court fees had not been paid, etc. In 166 cases divorce was finally decreed [4]. My intention was to obtain

[3] See on this p. 27.

[4] According to the Code of Civil Procedure, the final decree is a decree with respect to which no appeal may be brought. It is, in particular, a decree pronounced by the court of the first instance if no appeal has been brought within the time limit for appealing, as well as a decree pronounced, as result of an appeal, by the court of the second instance.

interviews in all the 166 cases. I succeeded in 78.9 per cent: 131 subjects were interviewed, 35 couples could not be reached due to mobility of the examined population, prolonged illness, refusals, etc.

These figures need some additional explanation. As I have said above, only one spouse was interviewed in each case. There were two reasons for this. First, if I had interviewed both, I would have been constrained, because of the expenses connected with interviewing, to a serious limitation of the number of couples interviewed; secondly, the losses would have been much higher: there were the court records which indicated that in 72 of the 166 couples above mentioned only one spouse lived in Cracow. In cases where both spouses lived in Cracow, I chose the subject to be interviewed not at random, but by means of considering, in the light of the court records, which of them would be more trustworthy or, in the second place, more inclined to speak; and if the contents of the records did not justify any assumption, I chose the woman, supposing that she would probably be more inclined to confide. Altogether 86 women and 45 men were interviewed.

The 131 interviews obtained this way were supplemented by two additional small samples. One of them was composed of interviews given by 8 of those divorced persons whose trials I had attended. These were the cases where there appeared a necessity for additional information besides the data made known in the courtroom. There were altogether 14 such cases. In 6 of them I did not succeed in obtaining an interview, in 8 I did. If both spouses lived in Cracow, the one who seemed, in the light of the court records, to be more trustworthy or more inclined to give an interview was chosen; if no such conjecture existed, the woman was interviewed. In this way 1 man and 7 women furnished information.

Another supplementary sample consisted of interviews of those who had become reconciled in the course of the divorce suit. This sample was drawn not from the suits attended by myself, but from those brought during the first 103 days of 1959, for its aim was to find out the effects of the court's conciliatory proceedings, and therefore the lapse of a fairly long period of time between reconciliation and the interview was necessary. The court records suggested altogether 29 possible reconciliations: withdrawals and suspensions of proceedings which might have been the effect of improved relations between the parties. Some of them were not interesting from the point of view of this study: in 13 cases the decision to withdraw the petition or to require suspension of proceedings had been made before the conciliatory session, which obviously means it was not an outcome of the conciliatory activity of the court. There remained 16 cases where it seemed that interviews would be useful: 10 withdrawals and 6 suspensions. I succeeded in obtaining 13 interviews: 8 after withdrawal and 5 after suspension. Here again I aimed at contacting the spouse who seemed to be more trustworthy and more inclined to give the interview, and in the absence of any conjecture – to contact the wife. This way 10 women and 2 men furnished information, and in one case both spouses in common.

All the interviews of divorced and reconciled persons were obtained between February and September, 1962. Each of them was preceded by a letter from the University, assuring secrecy. The interviewing was done by two sociologists experienced in such work. In order to assure that the recording of the information to be obtained should be as homogenous as possible, every point of the questionnaire was scrupulously discussed by the interviewers and myself.

For what reasons did the subjects interviewed furnish information? They were not asked about the reasons, but often made them known spontaneously. Some of them pointed out, in reference to content of the letter sent by the University, that they would like to render a service to scientific research. Some others hoped the interviewers would assist them in various difficulties resulting from divorce. It was obvious that many of them were guided by simple kindness. However, the most frequent motive was the need of confiding. Initially I had been afraid that the subjects interviewed would not be inclined to answer the questions, wishing to avoid speaking of confidential matters and returning to the painful past. This fear appeared, however, to be unjustified. A considerable number of them did not only answer the questions, but went beyond them and scrupulously described the most personal details. They were clearly pleased at having an opportunity of emotional purification, and sometimes, of giving vent to hatred of the former spouse. This inclination to detailed confidences, exceeding by far the intended scope of the interview, appeared in 44 interviews, of which 39 were given by women.

These reasons explain why in 93 cases (i.e. in 71.0 per cent of the sample) the interviewers were welcomed in a kind and friendly manner. This certainly had some influence on the credibility of interviews: the need of speaking does not guarantee sincerity, but it makes sincerity more probable. Moreover, the sincerity of the subjects interviewed was shown by various other symptoms. They often spontaneously assured the interviewer they would tell only the truth, and made a considerable effort to answer the questions exactly. Their appearance, way of presenting the case and the content of the information given were here important indications: reliability and sincerity were frequently striking, as is easily seen from numerous fragments of interviews quoted below. Sometimes the belief in the words of the subject interviewed was founded on his naiveté, on an impartial presentation of the marital conflict, on his making known his own blameworthy behaviour or the merits of the other spouse.

There were also other circumstances which justified belief in the credibility of the interviews. Here, in the first place, the content of the questions asked should be mentioned: they were not personal, which diminished the danger of deceitful answer. In particular, the interviewers did not ask about the causes of breakdown, and if the causes came out in many of the interviews, it was rather the result of an inclination to confide on the part of those interviewed, than an answer to the questions asked. Moreover, the veracity of the interviews, and to some degree also the scrupulousness of the interviewers, were constantly controlled by means of comparing the information furnished with contents of the court records. As I have said above, the records did not give a complete picture of the case, but they reproduced numerous elements exactly. With respect to the interviews these elements served in checking, and they, for the most part, confirmed the words of the subjects interviewed: this was the case when, e.g., the woman interviewed complained of her husband's drunkenness, and documents included in the records showed that he had undergone anti-alcoholic treatment; or, if she complained of delay in court, and the suit, indeed, had taken a long time. Lastly, there were also other circumstances indicating the veracity of the subjects interviewed. In some cases the interviewers obtained valuable information from the next-of-kin in the absence of the subject to be interviewed, and then, after the subject's return home, spoke with him. Many subjects showed various documents supporting their declarations: court decisions, letters, photographs.

The above does not indicate that all the interviews were fully trustworthy. There were also some factors which diminished their credibility. In some cases the interviewers recorded a reluctant attitude on the part of the subjects. In some others it was impossible to obtain the interview without the presence of third persons: the interviews were mostly given in the flats of those interviewed, usually densely inhabited. Some other difficulties also appeared: the haste of the subject, violent heat and anger, an inclination to exaggerate, fantasy, prevarications.

In effect, 1 interview was completely incredible, and a further 17 – partially so. The entirely incredible interview has been omitted, and I succeeded in obtaining the information from the spouse of the lying subject; the partially incredible remained in the sample, but were treated with particular caution.

2.6. These interviews were conducted, as I have said above, mainly to learn some antecedences and behind-the-scenes elements of the divorce suit. They were, however, limited to that part of the Cracow population which had been involved in divorce suits during the first 103 days of 1959. To extend the information in time and in space I drew on the experience of the 60 barristers interviewed. I asked all of them, in a general manner, about the antecedences and behind-the-scenes elements. Moreover, I asked 9 of the Cracow barristers about the antecedences and behind-the-scenes elements of some of the cases attended; I did it if such information appeared necessary in a given case, and I had good personal access to the barrister in charge of the case. Here again there arose the question of the credibility of the barristers' information. It was primarily a problem of the barristers' sincerity with respect to myself: I have presented above the means used to warrant it. Moreover, it was a question of the knowledge of the barristers themselves about the antecedences and behind-the-scenes elements of the cases in which they took part: it was far from clear to what degree the party informed his barrister about the elements of the case; and what would be the value of sincerity on the part of the barristers interviewed, if information obtained by them from their clients was incomplete or false. That was why it seemed necessary to check the barristers' knowledge. Two means were used to accomplish this: I asked the divorcees and the barristers themselves about it. The question put the divorcees was: "Was your barrister informed about the state of your marriage, and in particular about conflicts between you and spouse: very accurately – rather accurately – knew only some circumstances – did not know anything or hardly anything?". 81 of 131 divorcees interviewed had a barrister. Their answers were as in Table 2.

This table shows that the evident majority of the subjects interviewed informed their barristers very accurately. This conclusion has been confirmed by information furnished by barristers from Warsaw, Cracow, Lublin and Katowice. All of them were asked: "Do you think that a party in a divorce suit always informs – usually informs – only sometimes informs his barrister about the main circumstances indicating

TABLE 2

Opinion of the Parties on the Barristers' Knowledge of the Marital Conflict

Answers	Number of Subjects	% %
very accurately	55	67.9
rather accurately	13	16.1
knew only some circumstances	12	14.8
did not know anything or hardly anything	1	1.2
TOTALS	81	100.0

the degree and permanency of marital failure?". The putting of this question seemed to be justified: the barristers not only have some intuition as to the veracity and completeness of the information obtained, but, moreover, have at their disposal a special kind of test: if this information is false or partial only, they frequently learn it in the courtroom, in the course of collecting evidence. Their answers were as follows:

TABLE 3

Opinion of Barristers on Their Knowledge of Conflict between the Parties

Answers	Number of Subjects	% %
always informs	14	23.3
usually informs	41	68.4
only sometimes informs	2	3.3
no answer	3	5.0
TOTALS	60	100.0

Thus, in the light of the figures here presented, it seems to be a safe guess that the barristers are usually accurately informed about the state of their clients' marriage.

2.7. The above data had to be supplemented in some ways. There appeared, mainly in order to be able to evaluate the recrimination rule, the necessity of some public opinion research. In this I was helped by the Public Opinion Research Centre in Warsaw which, in 1962, interviewed a sample of 2,355 subjects, representative of the whole country. However, these last interviews were not sufficient: it appeared in the pilot study that some of the questions which I had intended to include in the questionnaire were too difficult for the average respondent. To answer them I interviewed an additional sample of 323 evening students of law at the University of Cracow; a detailed analysis of the way in which the sample was drawn and of the information furnished due to its drawing will be presented below. Lastly, I used published as well as unpublished statistical data collected by the Ministry of Justice and by the Central Statistical Office.

2.8. To conclude this chapter, let me present the symbols to be used to denote the collected data:

1. The main sample of trials attended: T-1 – 153
2. The surplus sample of trials attended: S-1 – 34
3. The conciliatory sessions attended: CS-1 – 84
4. The main sample of interviews of the divorced persons: D-1 – 131
5. Interviews of those who obtained divorce in the course of the trials attended: DA-1 – 8
6. Interviews of the reconciled persons: R-1 – 13
7. Interviews of judges: J-1 – 41
8. Interviews of barristers: B-1 – 60
9. Interviews of students: ST-1 – 323

III

THE PROVISIONS IN FORCE

One cannot present the working of any legal institution without at least an elementary description of the provisions in force: hence the following comments concerning the Polish divorce law. Since, however, the same legislative model has been adopted by all the East European divorce laws, these remarks can also be applied to all of them, subject to a few rather secondary differences.

The family law was changed in Poland in the course of preparing this study: the Family Code of 1950 has been superseded by the Family and Guardianship Code, promulgated in 1964, in force since January 1, 1965. However, the divorce provisions of the new code follow the former ones word for word, or contain only unimportant changes.

Art. 56 Para. 1 of the new code, following Art. 29 Para. 1 of the old one, determines that "if a marriage has completely and permanently broken down, either spouse may demand of the court the dissolution of the marriage by divorce". It is, however, the duty of the court not only to examine the degree and permanency of breakdown and to pronounce divorce or dismiss the petition according to the results of the inquiry; its duty is also to attempt to reconcile the spouses. At the beginning of each suit the parties are to be called to a conciliatory session, where the judge in charge shall induce them "to become reconciled, in consideration of the welfare of the children and the social import of durability of marriage"; only "if the appearance of either party involves substantial difficulties..., may the court forego the conciliatory session". The court should also, in the further course of the trial, "induce the parties to reconciliation if it finds reconciliation practicable". Moreover, if the court "comes to the conclusion that there is a chance of preserving the marriage union, the proceedings should be suspended", and if within one year thereafter [1] neither

[1] Before 1965 the elapse of three years was necessary.

party requires the court to resume the proceedings, the extinction of the suit comes about (Arts. 223 Para. 1, 436 Para. 1, 437, 440 of the Code of Civil Procedure).

The above quoted basic provision, allowing the pronouncement of divorce in the event of complete and permanent breakdown of marriage, has been seriously limited in the current as well as in the previous law. The first of the limitations was introduced in the interests of the child: "in spite of complete and permanent breakdown..., divorce cannot be decreed, if as a result the welfare of the infant children of both parties would suffer" (Art. 56 Para. 2 of the Family and Guardianship Code, following the previous Art. 29 Para. 2). The second was introduced by the rule of recrimination. According to Art. 30 of the former Family Code of 1950, "divorce cannot be decreed if the petitioner alone is guilty of the breakdown, unless the defendant consents to divorce" (Para. 1); however, even in default of such consent, the court may..., "having regard for the social interest, decree divorce, provided that the spouses have long lived apart" (Para. 2). According to Art. 56 Para. 3 of the present Family and Guardianship Code, "divorce cannot be decreed... if the petitioner alone is guilty of the breakdown of the marriage unless either the respondent consents to divorce or the refusal of his consent is, in the given circumstances, contrary to the principles of social co-operation" [2]. This provision is strictly connected with another: "when pronouncing the divorce decree the court shall determine whether either of the spouses, and which of them, or neither, is guilty of the breakdown of the marriage..., however, on the unanimous request of both spouses the court shall refrain from deciding the question of guilt", and "the effects of such a case are as if neither spouse were guilty" (Art. 57 of the Family and Guardianship Code of 1964, following art. 31 of the Family Code of 1950). This last provision indicates that, in the event of the unilateral guilt of the petitioner, consent of his spouse may be given in two ways: it can either be a consent to divorce brought about by the petitioner's guilt or consent to divorce without deciding the question of guilt.

The above provisions gave rise to controversies as to their meaning.

[2] The expression "principles of social co-operation" has been substituted, in the contemporary Polish law, for the traditional expressions: "principles of good faith", "principles of public order", "decent customs". The meaning of the "principles of social co-operation" has been the subject of divergent views expressed in various decisions of the Supreme Court, and by several legal writers. According to the prevailing opinion, this expression denotes, in particular, the rules of socialist morality.

Two of them seem to be worth mentioning. The first concerns the concept of "breakdown of marriage", the second – welfare of the infant child.

Since the working of norms on breakdown of marriage constitutes the subject of this study, it seems to be indispensable to ascertain in what meaning the word "breakdown" will be used. Its meaning is far from being clear, and at least three suggestions have been put forward on this. According to the first of them, breakdown of marriage means a psychic phenomenon: decline of those feelings of which marital unity is usually composed. According to the second, considering marital unity as composed not only of feelings, but also, and even mainly, various kinds of behaviour, the word "breakdown" denotes not only default of affection, but also behaviour of the spouses contrary to that usual in a working marriage union. Some others propose that breakdown means nonperformance of marital duties. Any detailed presentations or critical analysis of those suggestions, the practical effects of which hardly differ from each other, would exceed the requirements of this study. That is why I shall limit myself to explaining the meaning in which the expression "breakdown of marriage" will be used below.

It will be used in the meaning indicated by numerous decisions of the Supreme Court, in particular by its guide lines [3] of 1955, for, in this meaning the expression "breakdown of marriage" is simple, nearly colloquial, and, on the other hand, it is defined to the necessary degree. Moreover, it is known in this meaning to judges and barristers: I have asked them in the interviews about various questions connected with breakdown, and I therefore had to use this expression in a meaning familiar to them. According to the guide lines of 1955 "the marital unity consists of a peculiar kind of emotional, physical and economic partnership. The ceasing of any element of this partnership should, in principle, be considered as a symptom of breakdown of marriage... However, the ceasing of physical or economic partnership does not necessarily constitute a symptom of breakdown, if it results from circumstances independent of the spouses", such as disease, stay in hospital, absence on duty, etc. "On the other hand default of emotional partnership (the existence of which may come out if only in correspondence) is always a symptom of breakdown... Its default may be stated even without a hostile or unfriendly mutual attitude. Preserving of correct

[3] The guide lines of the Supreme Court – an institution unknown to the Western legal systems – contain instructions, binding the lower courts, on interpretation and application of legal provisions.

mutual relations, remaining in contact because of interests of the common children, etc., does not necessarily mean that emotional partnership between the spouses has been maintained... For, not any... partnership between two persons, but a partnership characteristic of the marriage union is here at stake".[4]

The breakdown is complete if "all the links between the spouses have been severed" [5]; i.e. if "the emotional, physical and economic partnership does not exist" any more [6], obviously subject to the above provisions. The requirement that the breakdown be permanent does not mean "complete impossibility" of return to a common life [7]. If this were its meaning, the court would have to predict with certainty the future relations of the parties, which is not possible. It is sufficient if, in the light of a knowledge of the world, their return seems improbable [8].

So much as to the meaning of "breakdown of marriage". Another problem of import which gave rise to divergent opinions is the welfare of the child as a factor hindering pronouncement of divorce. Two views have been set forth on this point. According to the first the child's welfare, as a rule, requires the dismissal of the petition for divorce; consequently, if the spouses have infant children, divorce may be pronounced only in exceptional cases [9]. According to the second, divorce in a case of broken marriage usually has no undesirable impact on the child's situation, for which reason a petition for divorce may hardly be dismissed because of the child's welfare [10]. Those holding such fixed opinions declare them categorically, but without giving convincing reasons. Yet, this controversy can be decided by means of empirical investigations, in particular by a skilful comparison of a sample of children of broken but not divorced families with a sample of children

[4] Resolution of the whole Civil Chamber of the Supreme Court of 28 April 1955, I Co 5/55.

[5] Decree of the Supreme Court of 5 January 1952, C.431/51.

[6] The guide lines of 1955, section II/1.

[7] The guide lines of 1955, section II/2.

[8] Decree of the Supreme Court of 13 January 1953, C.1631/52.

[9] A. Stelmachowski, "Dobro dziecka w procesie rozwodowym" ("The Welfare of the Child in the Divorce Suit") in *Nowe Prawo* (1953/8-9), p. 58 et seq.

[10] M. Wawiłowa, "Jeszcze o interesie dziecka w procesie rozwodowym" ("Some More Remarks on the Interest of the Child in the Divorce Suit") in *Nowe Prawo* (1964/2), p. 49 et seq.; S. Garlicki, "Dobro małoletnich dzieci jako negatywna przesłanka rozwodowa" ("The Welfare of the Minor Children as a Circumstance Hindering Pronouncement of Divorce") in *Nowe Prawo* (1955/5), p. 51 et seq.

of divorcees; it would, however, require further research extending beyond the limits of the present study.

In conclusion – some final information, concerning the problem of procedure mentioned above. There are three grades of courts in Poland: county courts, voivodship courts and the Supreme Court. Till 1958 the voivodship courts tried the divorce cases in the first instance, and the Supreme Court in appeal. However, because of considerable caseload and delays in the Supreme Court, divorce cases were transferred, on July 12, 1958, to the competence of 44 county courts as first instance; appeals go to the voivodship courts. This resulted in the shortening of suits; but, on the other hand, it also did away with the decisions of the Supreme Court which had, up till then, acted as sign posts in divorce cases. The decisions of this court mentioned in this work were issued in the suits filed before July, 1958.

IV

BREAKDOWN OF MARRIAGE

1. GOALS AND CONJECTURES

The legislator who considers the principle on which divorce is to be granted meets with several patterns in the laws of various countries. Two of them are encountered more frequently than others. First, the doctrine of matrimonial offence, according to which certain acts of a particularly grave nature are regarded as incompatible with the duties undertaken on entering into marriage. The committing of these acts by one spouse entitles the other to claim divorce: this standpoint has, in principle, been adopted by the majority of the divorce laws in Western Europe and North America. The principle of breakdown constitutes the second pattern: it allows divorce to be granted if the marriage has irretrievably broken down.

There are countries in Eastern Europe which have not only followed the second of these two basic patterns, but have adopted, in a somewhat uncompromising manner, the breakdown of marriage as an all-embracing ground for divorce. This has been the position in the Soviet family law, since 1949, when the Soviet Supreme Court set down the guide lines on the practice of the courts in divorce cases. This also became, at the turn of the '40 s, the position of the family laws in Poland, Czechoslovakia, Hungary, Bulgaria and Rumania.

There are two fundamental purposes for which the socialist countries in Eastern Europe rejected the doctrine of matrimonial offence. They appear clearly in the light of declarations of East European legislative bodies, supreme courts and legal writers. The first of these aims is to assure a more liberal access to divorce. It may happen that neither spouse has committed any of the offences mentioned in a given legal system, but nevertheless the marriage has become, because of other circumstances, a complete failure: let the spouses be free to dissolve their union in such a case as well. To express the idea more broadly:

whenever a marriage is completely broken down, let the spouses be free to dissolve their union [1], without respect to the cause of failure, even in the absence of any definite fault on the part of either party.

This liberal attitude seems to be an effect of a rational legislative approach supported by wide historic experience. The granting of divorce in a limited number of definite matrimonial offences, and, above all, limiting them to a few acts of a particularly grave nature, makes it impossible to dissolve those broken marriages in which no fault constituting ground for divorce has been committed, and, consequently, prevents the spouses from dissolving an unhappy union; and maintaining of unhappy unions against the parties' will results in hardship and frustration.

The hardship and frustration create a desire to end a broken marriage so strong that it frequently leads, in the absence of legal remedies, to dishonest dissolutions of the marriage bonds. Here the least scrupulous are most successful. Thus, under those legislations in which divorce is either very difficult or unknown, the tendency towards dishonest annulment of marriages appears: it has appeared in Italy, it appeared, in the years 1918–1939, in those parts of Poland where Catholic marriages could not be ended by divorce, and, until 1966, in New York where, according to the data for the years 1940–1948, annulments, a high proportion of them sham, amounted to almost one third of the United States total [2]. Another abuse resulting from narrow grounds for divorce is the producing of bogus grounds. Change of religion and migratory divorce are other remedies: change of religion appears under those systems which make divorce dependent on the religious affiliation of the spouses, migratory divorce mainly in countries divided into various legal areas of which some are more, and others less, liberal with respect to divorce.

Thus life appears stronger than restrictive provisions. Hence the tendency toward less rigorous restrictions which has become influential not only recently in New York, but also, much earlier, under certain other rigorous legal systems. In France divorce had been unknown since 1816, and was introduced in 1884, *inter alia* on the grounds of adultery, imprisonment, cruelty, intolerable conduct. The French courts interpreted "cruelty" and "intolerable conduct", despite a restrictive

[1] Of course, provided that the welfare of the child and (under some of the East European family laws) the rule of recrimination do not contradict divorce.

[2] W. Gellhorn, *Children and Families in the Courts of New York City* (1954), p. 274.

legislative correction of 1941, in a liberal and broad manner, and the Cour de Cassation accepts this interpretation [3]. The evolution of English law tended in the same direction. In England adultery had long been the only ground for divorce. It was only the Matrimonial Causes Act of 1937 that introduced further grounds: cruelty, desertion, insanity, i.e. circumstances which had formerly justified separation only. The English law did not, however, limit itself to this: the courts have interpreted the terms "cruelty" and "desertion" broadly, and the tendency towards ascribing them a still broader meaning continues [4], "for the circumstances which might conceivably arise in an unhappy married life are infinitely various" [5].

However, even this relaxation of the system, being but a palliative, has proved inadequate: the grounds for divorce are still, in relation to the number of broken marriages, too narrow, which results in abuses such as the deliberate or pretended committing of matrimonial offences in order to supply grounds for divorce. In the opinion of Professor Gower, "among the upper income groups... it is well over half the total of undefended cases... which may be regarded as collusive or based on bogus grounds" [6]; and the undefended cases make up about 90 per cent of the total [7]. Hence the views of some of the members of the Morton Commission who think "that the law of divorce as it at present exists is indeed weighted in favour of the least scrupulous, the least honourable and the least sensitive"; and that "nobody who is ready to provide a ground of divorce... has any difficulty in securing a dissolution of the marriage" [8]; which "brings the whole administration of the law into disrepute" [9].

It is not surprising, in the light of the experience here presented, that the idea of enabling the spouses to obtain divorce whenever their union becomes a complete failure has been adopted by all the lawmakers in Eastern Europe. It has also been adopted by some of the West European family laws: West German, Austrian, Swiss. However,

[3] A. Colin, H. Capitant, J. de la Morandière, *Traité de droit civil*, vol. I (1957), p. 685 et seq.

[4] L. Rosen, "Cruelty in Matrimonial Causes", *Modern Law Review* (1949), p. 324; O. Kahn-Freund, "Divorce Law Reform?", *Modern Law Review* (1956), pp. 586, 587.

[5] Words of Lord Simons in Watt v. Thomas, [1947] 1 All E.R.582, p. 585.

[6] Quoted after O.R. Mc Gregor, *Divorce in England* (1957), p. 135.

[7] O.R. Mc Gregor, *ibid.*

[8] *Report of the Royal Commission on Marriage and Divorce* (1956), Cmd. 70/5.

[9] Words of Professor Gower, quoted after O.R. Mc Gregor, *ibid.*

in contradistinction to Germany, Austria, Switzerland, where breakdown constitutes, along with various matrimonial offences, one of the grounds, under the East European legal systems it became an all-embracing ground for divorce, not supplementing, but completely ruling out the offences: no matrimonial offence justifies pronouncement of divorce if not resulting in marital failure. This disposition has as its aim the second fundamental purpose of those legal systems, to let the spouses dissolve their union *only* where the breakdown of their marriage has indeed appeared complete and permanent.

This second purpose is the outcome of a more general, restrictive tendency, which is against the obtaining of divorces too easily. Several arguments have been brought forward in favour of this tendency, mainly the effect of marital failure on the spouses and on their children. For the spouses it is a source of suffering. Its unfavourable impact on the development of the child is, in particular, caused by the fact that the parents' living apart usually results in the loss of one of them, while, because of their different abilities and attitudes, they are both necessary to the child during its period of growth and adaptation. It is, for the most part, the loss of the father, whom the child needs "as an object of love, security or identification or even as a figure against whom to rebel safely". When the absence of the parent is caused by marital failure and not death, "the psychodynamic structure of the child is further complicated by hostilities and guilts for hostility, by feelings of abandonment, and by guilts for divided loyalties" [10]. These effects result from breakdown of marriage, and, if in a given case the breakdown is indeed complete and permanent, no provisions of the divorce law can prevent them. Nevertheless, if the legislator allowed divorce without breakdown, on the ground of matrimonial offence only, he would produce those effects himself. For, it frequently happens that, despite the committing of an offence, the marriage continues to work: in those events the acceptance of the doctrine of matrimonial offence leads to marriages being dissolved where, if the law were other, a common life could probably continue, whereas introduction of the principle of breakdown as an all-embracing ground for divorce prevents the dissolution of working marriages.

A further argument frequently used against too easy divorce is the view that "divorce breeds divorce". This means that the granting of divorce for a wide range of reasons favours the breakdown of marriages

[10] W. J. Goode, *After Divorce* (1956), p. 309.

and results in an extensive increase of resort to divorce. This opinion, widespread in various countries, is supported by certain more detailed conjectures. First, it is believed that facility in getting a divorce results in a tendency to enter into marriage more lightly, and in a marriage thus lightly contracted the probability of breakdown, and, in effect, of divorce, grows. Moreover, the more difficult it is to obtain divorce under a given legal system, the greater will be the efforts of the spouses to avoid conflicts: they will be induced to those efforts by the necessity of continuing a marriage union which cannot easily be dissolved. Furthermore, divorce suits are the more frequently brought when it is easier to obtain divorce, and the bringing of a divorce suit aggravates the existing conflict, due to its embittering influence. It sometimes makes a complete failure of a marriage which could otherwise be reconciled. According to an opinion encountered among American writers, the rise of the divorce rate increases the number of divorced persons in the marriage market, which results in a better chance of remarriage of all those before whom the prospect of divorce appears, and this is an additional inducement to divorce. Moreover, numerous divorces in a given community are supposed to give rise to a "process of social imitation" similar to such phenomena as "mass conversions, inflation and panic behaviour" [11]; lastly, the growth of the divorce rate is supposed to cause danger to the marriages of future generations: the children of parents who have been granted divorce show a more-than-chance tendency to appear in the divorce court themselves, which can be explained by "the taking of parental roles in childhood and introjection of parental attitudes toward divorce" [12].

These are the reasons for which all the family laws in Eastern Europe have aimed at limiting divorce to those cases in which the breakdown of marriage appears complete and permanent. This aim has been pointed out frequently and emphatically. According to the above-mentioned guide lines issued in 1949 by the Soviet Supreme Court, "the courts must take into account that no temporary family discord or... conflicts between the spouses may be regarded as sufficient grounds for divorce. A marriage may be dissolved only if... there is, in the event of its continuance... no possibility of the spouses living together and bringing up the children" [13]. This idea has been developed by the

[11] C. Kirkpatrick, *The Family as Process and Institution* (1955), p. 522.
[12] *Ibid.*
[13] The guide lines of the Full Assembly of the Soviet Supreme Court on the court practice in the divorce suits, issued September 16, 1949.

subsequent Soviet court decisions [14] and by Soviet legal writers; "the only ground for divorce is breakdown of marriage and impossibility of restoration of a common life" [15]. This has also become the viewpoint of the law-makers and court decisions in all the people's democracies, among them Poland: "divorce may be decreed only if the court states complete and permanent breakdown of marriage" [16], and in the event of unjustified pronouncement of divorce "an infringement of the social interest" is committed [17]; for, marital stability can be secured "only if divorce is founded on the principle of breakdown" [18], so that it may be decreed only where "the marriage union is unworkable" [19]. "That is why the court is bound in each divorce suit to learn whether breakdown actually exists" [20], and whether it is, indeed, complete and permanent [21].

The feasibility of the first of the two legislative purposes under discussion – whenever a marriage is completely and permanently broken, let the spouses be free to dissolve their union – did not arouse much interest: it is commonly considered that, under those laws which accept breakdown of marriage as ground for divorce, this purpose is being realized, and if any difficulties appear in its achievement, they result from various social pressures about which more will be said below, and on which the provisions of the divorce law cannot have any serious influence. On the other hand, the feasibility of the second fundamental purpose – let the spouses dissolve their union only when the breakdown of their marriage is indeed complete and permanent – has given rise to doubt: it is a widespread belief that it is hardly possible to realize this purpose. This conviction is to be encountered wherever the problem of introducing the principle of breakdown into the divorce law appears, and it has been clearly emphasized by those members of the Morton Commission opposed to the introduction of that principle. In their

[14] G. M. Svierdlov, *Sovetskoje siemiejnoje pravo (Soviet Family Law)* (1951), pp. 90-92.

[15] A. I. Piergament in D. M. Genkin and S. N. Bratus, ed., *Sovetskoje grazdanskoje pravo (Soviet Civil Law)*, vol. II (1951), p. 397.

[16] Decree of the Supreme Court of 21 May, 1949, WaC. 30/49.

[17] Decree of the Supreme Court of 31 October, 1952, C.1820/51.

[18] J. Gwiazdomorski, M. Grudzinski, S. Kaleta, A. Wolter, "Załozenia prawa rodzinnego w swietle konstytucji PRL" ("Premises of the Family Law in the Light of Polish Constitution") in *Zagadnienia prawne konstytucji PRL (The Legal Problems of the Constitution of People's Republic of Poland)*, vol. III (1954), p. 65.

[19] S. Szer, *Prawo rodzinne (Family Law)* (1957), p. 108.

[20] The guide lines of 1955 (see above, p. 26, footnote 4).

[21] Decree of the Supreme Court of 22 February, 1952, C.681/51.

opinion its acceptance "would set the court an impossible task. To determine whether or not a marriage had completely broken down is really not a triable issue. If the case were undefended and the petitioner maintained he would never go back to his spouse, and that the marriage was dead, and if his statements were perhaps supported by evidence of his relatives and friends", the court could not "do otherwise than... grant a divorce. This would mean that many divorces would in reality be given merely on the ground of incompatibility" and "that it would be open to husband and wife to obtain divorce by consent". In effect people would "come to look upon marriage less and less as a life-long union", and "in the end widespread divorce would come to be an accepted feature of our society", which "would undermine, and ultimately destroy, the concept of life-long marriage" [22].

It is interesting that in Eastern Europe, and particularly in Poland, the introduction of the principle of breakdown gave rise to similar views. Complaints are to be heard that, as a result of the too liberal attitude of the courts, divorce is not limited to cases of complete and permanent marital failure. The complaints concern in particular the uncontested cases, which constitute a high proportion of the divorce suits; in a considerable number of them "it seems probable that the courts... are not scrupulous enough in finding out whether all the legal requirements for pronouncement of divorce have been fulfilled" [23]. For, in this kind of case, the courts usually limit themselves "to accepting the parties' statements as to the causes of breakup, and find the defendant's consent conclusive for pronouncement of divorce. Thus, the deciding of such cases becomes... a formality consisting in taking the parties' declarations that they unanimously request" divorce, regardless of the fact that "requirements concerning complete and permanent breakdown of marriage" should be fulfilled [24]. In the opinion of some legal writers the introduction of the principle of breakdown, practically speaking, comes near to being divorce by consent [25].

[22] Report........., Cmd.69/II, XXXIV.

[23] T. Dybowski, "Niektóre zagadnienia problematyki rozwodowej na tle orzecznictwa" ("Some Divorce Problems in the Light of Court Practice") in *Nowe Prawo* (1965/6), p. 60.

[24] M. Gintowt, "Rozwodowe refleksje" ("Reflections on Divorce") in *Prawo i Zycie* (1960 / 1), p. 3.

[25] J. Wasilkowski, A. Wolter, "Wyniki publicznej dykusji nad projektem kodeksu cywilnego" ("Results of a Public Discussion on the Draft Civil Code") in *Prawo i Zycie* (1961/22), p. 3.

How true are these conjectures? Does the acceptance of the principle of breakdown indeed result in the above dangers? Are the courts really unable to learn the degree and permanency of breakdown, and, in consequence, to limit divorce to the events where breakdown of marriage has become complete and permanent? Only far-reaching empirical investigations carried out in countries where breakdown of marriage has become an all-embracing ground for divorce may contribute to finding the answers to these questions. Let me present the results of the inquiry arranged in Poland.

2. CAUSES AND SYMPTOMS OF BREAKDOWN

2.1. The court can state the occurrence of breakdown, and estimate its completeness and permanency, by learning two groups of circumstances. First – the causes of breakdown, i.e. the facts which explain its occurrence and, if they are important, make the breakdown probable. Secondly, the symptoms of breakdown, i.e. the apparent behaviour of the spouses which indicates its occurrence and degree. Here, however, a comment on terminology should be made. The words "cause" and "symptom" are here so used that their scopes are crossed, not opposed to each other; very frequently the same fact – an act of cruelty, desertion, concubinage – is a factor contributing to the occurrence or growth of breakdown, and, simultaneously, a symptom of it. Moreover, the term "cause" has here a meaning differing from that commonly accepted. Usually causes are opposed to effects; here however, the distinction is not always clear. Sometimes it is: if a wife, having learned that her husband had committed a criminal offence before marriage, deserts him, the offence certainly is the cause of breakdown, not its effect. Still, dubious situations frequently occur: neurotic temper, sexual maladjustment, adultery, alcoholism, may be causes or symptoms; and they are very often simultaneously both – a feedback, to use a term drawn from cybernetics – because, causing the conflict, they subsequently grow stronger under its influence or, being an effect of the conflict, they eventually result in its growth.

2.2. Breakdown of marriage is never an outcome of one particular circumstance, in spite of the fact that the court records may sometimes suggest it is; the records furnish instances of breakdown caused allegedly only by single facts such as adultery or desertion. Breakdown of marriage is always an effect of a multitude of factors, psychological and social [26].

It is not always necessary for the court to learn of these factors in order to ascertain whether, in a given case, the breakdown is indeed complete and permanent. Such knowledge is needless where the symptoms make the existence of breakdown evident. The trials observed furnished instances of this, mostly in cases of long separation [27]: in 13 trials over 8 years, of which 6 cases lasted from 16 to 32 years, the separation was usually accompanied by longstanding concubinage on the part of one or both spouses, and in 8 of the 13 prolonged separations mentioned, children were born in concubinage. Thus, in trial T-71, the defendant had deserted his wife and daughter in 1946, and he was not heard of for 7 years; in 1953 he wrote a short letter from Canada, and in the next letter, written 4 years later, in reply to the daughter's wedding announcement, he asked them not to write to him because he would be moving to an unknown destination. In case T-98 the plaintiff had deserted his wife in 1953, and then they both entered into concubinage; the wife gave birth to a child with her new partner, and the plaintiff had two children with the concubine and looked after them carefully. He sued for divorce in order to marry their mother. In case T-107 the parties married in 1954; immediately after marriage the plaintiff, without starting cohabitation with his wife, began his military service, and, after release from the army, never returned to her. In case T-142 the parties left each other in 1931, and, after 30 years of separation, the plaintiff filed a petition for divorce, intending to marry his concubine with whom he had a 22-year-old son. It seems that in all these and similar cases the symptoms of breakdown are, even without detailed examination of its causes, sufficient to show that the breakdown has become complete and that the return of the spouses to a common life is not probable.

2.3. These cases are, however, a minority: for the most part the examination of causes appears necessary, and sometimes only a detailed and scrupulous analysis of them enables the court to evaluate properly

[26] See on this in particular the seminal studies of L. M. Terman (*Psychological Factors in Marital Happiness*, 1938), E. W. Burgess and L. S. Cottrell (*Predicting Success or Failure in Marriage*, 1939), H. J. Locke (*Predicting Adjustment in Marriage: A Comparison of a Divorced and a Happily Married Group*, 1951), and others – which indicate how numerous these factors are.

[27] The word "separation" here means simply the living apart of the spouses; the separation after court order is unknown in Poland, as in all the countries of Eastern Europe.

the degree and permanency of breakdown. Not only observation of trials, but also, and even more, interviewing of divorced persons confirmed the point: some of the divorced revealed that the court, not having examined the causes of breakdown properly, had evaluated its degree and permanency in a dubious or even erroneous manner. Thus, in case D-73, according to the words of the defendant wife registered in the court record, the plaintiff had raped her and coerced her into cohabitation; the effect of that behaviour was her pregnancy and marriage, after which the plaintiff used to beat, insult and maltreat her. On the other hand, according to his statements, she had lived with him before marriage without any coercion, and after marriage displayed a quarrelsome temper. The court pronounced divorce, and in an interview given by her she confessed that the rape and coercion had been sham, and the real factors, hidden from the court, had been her immaturity and lack of experience, as well as her submissiveness to her mother, who was domineering and ill-disposed towards her husband. However, the influence of those factors was probably not really strong, since she told the interviewer that if the court had dismissed the petition for divorce, they would possibly have been reconciled: "possibly now, being older and more experienced, I would know how to live with him"; she felt this was also her husband's opinion: he did not marry again, "is not interested in any other woman", and "deplores divorce". In case D-98, according to the statements registered in the court record, the parties had left each other because of incompatibility of characters, and the plaintiff entered into concubinage. The interview given by his wife indicated that he had deserted her during the war. The parties accidentally met a few years later and decided to become reconciled; however, after a short time, he left her again. She subsequently found him, with a concubine, in a distant town. He then returned to her, but eventually requested divorce. In spite of the fact that divorce had been granted, he did not marry the concubine, and, in the opinion of the wife interviewed, if the court had dismissed the petition for divorce, the marriage "would certainly have been brought to agreement": the former husband is tender to her, he assures her of his affection, "writes letters which are as warm as if they were written to the most beloved mistress, sends gifts, invites me to visit him"; she explains this odd behaviour by the weakness of his character, probably "that woman blackmails him and he is unable to disentangle himself, he is at bottom a good man, but very weak". In case D-100 the unfaithfulness of the defendant wife was given in court as the cause of breakdown. In the interview, however, the husband made it known that the conflict had been an outcome of various factors, in particular of the difference between the social backgrounds of the parties, difference in age, harmful impact of in-laws, and his own traumas. The court did not learn all these factors, and, consequentially, was unable to evaluate their import. Divorce had been decreed, and shortly after its pronouncement the parties became reconciled, and continued cohabitation. It is possible that a more detailed analysis of the causes of conflict would have prevented pronouncement of divorce.

3. CIRCUMSTANCES HINDERING THE COURT IN LEARNING THE CAUSES AND SYMPTOMS OF BREAKDOWN

3.1. The court is frequently unable to learn exactly the causes and symptoms of marital failure. One of the reasons for this is the fact that the court takes into account, in principle, the data and evidence offered by the parties; the real causes of breakdown are often unknown to the spouses themselves. This want of knowledge has been conclusively confirmed in marriage counselling practice, a social service just starting its activities in Poland, but long known in many other countries. The experience of the marriage counselling centres indicates that the spouses are often unable themselves to discern the very roots of conflict. This is only a centre – and it is one of its important functions – which should enable people "to understand better their own basic experiences, feelings, desires, anxieties and inadequacies", as well as "the general character structure of their... mates" [28], and, consequently, lead them "to see the situation clearly" so that they should not try "to cure their marital troubles on the basis of a false diagnosis" [29].

This does not mean, however, that the parties do not know anything: they usually are familiar with some elements resulting in conflict, and, as result, even certain deeply hidden psychological or social roots of breakdown are often brought to light in the courtroom. Thus a defendant whose childhood had been spent, during the war, in extreme misery, was shocked by the contrast between his wife's wealth and his own poverty; the disgust increased due to his religious fanaticism, and the

[28] A. Ellis, "A Critical Evaluation of Marriage Counseling", *"Marriage and Family Living"* (1956), p. 67.

[29] R. Mace, *Marriage Counselling* (The First Full Account of the Remedial Work of the Marriage Guidance Council) (1948), p. 68.

wedding reception given by her was, in his opinion, "luxury beyond bearing"; moreover, he believed the mere fact of getting married was disloyalty to his mother (S-3). In another case there appeared in the court a couple which, because of pregnancy, had married in the state of complete emotional immaturity. The parties revealed the husband's unhappy childhood: he deserted his hated parental home where he had been given no affection. After getting married he was so jealous that he forbade the wife to leave the house, and phoned her, from his job, several times a day to check whether she was in. Moreover, as she told the court, crying, he wanted to buy her "a red overcoat and red shoes in order to make me look like his former girl-friend" (T-36). In case S-2 the husband knew that he did not sexually satisfy his wife; therefore he obsessively suspected her of being faithless, and behaved vulgarly towards her, in particular after disappointing relations; then he apologised. Moreover, he used to drink, and told the court, explaining his inclination to alcohol: "I have a fatal character, my parents' marriage was a failure, I lived a hell of a life at home from early childhood, and am not adjusted to conjugal life". These instances might be multiplied; the parties themselves frequently call the attention of the court to their immaturity at the time of marriage, difference in social background, bad influence of their own childhood, sexual inhibitions, neurotic or psychopathic personality traits. However, even when doing so, they reveal an incomplete image; being conscious only of some, not of all the factors contributing to the occurrence and growth of breakdown, they are unable to present all of them in the courtroom.

3.2. This is, however, not the only source of lack of knowledge on the part of the court. Its source is also, and mainly, the attitude of the parties who often do not want to let the court know the symptoms of breakdown or those causes of breakdown which are known to themselves. They deceive the court, hiding the real causes and symptoms, and presenting the sham. The variety of reasons for which they behave in this way appeared in the interviews. Many of the divorcees interviewed gave as the reason a feeling of shame and dislike of revealing confidential affairs: "if I told the court that my husband had such a filthy thing I would be ill with shame" said a woman interviewed who had divorced her husband mainly because of his venereal disease (D-51); the husband disaffected to his wife because of an abortion did not reveal it in the court in order to avoid the "washing of dirty linen in public" (D-84); in another case all the statements contained in the petition were fictitious: "I went with my former husband to a barrister with whom we were acquainted", and to hide our personal affairs, "we three thought up various charges" (DA-4). Sometimes this reason is connected with the desire to avoid hurting the feelings of the other spouse: "my wife had asked me, before we came to the court, not to tell about all that, because she didn't want to be shamed, and I would have been ashamed as well, for she had my surname, and, in fact, she was just a prostitute" (D-15); "I had to say something against my wife, and I didn't want to..., my barrister told me I wouldn't succeed without saying it, but, despite his advice, I didn't say anything against her in the court" (D-24). Sometimes there appeared a wish to make the best impression on the court: to justify my own faults "I charged my wife with adultery, but the charge was groundless" (D-4). The fear of criminal liability may also play a role: "I didn't tell that as a result of my husband's behaviour I had 13 abortions, because I had been told by him that if the court learned it, my doctors would be accused and I would also get into trouble" (D-107). There also appeared some other reasons: according to the information furnished by one of the women interviewed, the parties presented a fictitious cause of breakdown in court, because telling the truth could have had a harmful influence upon her professional career (D-12).

However, none of these motives is so frequent as reasons of procedural tactics: the parties hide the real causes and symptoms, and present the court the fictitious ones, in order to achieve the goals aimed at in the divorce suit. Three of these goals are of particular import. First – obtaining of divorce, or of dismissal: its achievement depends upon causes and symptoms, because they show the degree and permanency of marital failure, and, moreover, the causes indicate whether the plaintiff has not been solely guilty of the breakdown. The second of the procedural goals is the obtaining of the desired decision as to who is guilty of the breakdown: this depends upon the causes of breakdown, because the causes indicate which spouse, if any, is guilty. The third aim is to obtain the desired decision as to the custody of the common child or children; here, however, the reasons for which the parties deceive the court are more complex.

According to Art. 58 of the Family and Guardianship Code, being tantamount to a provision contained in the previous Family Code, "in the divorce decree the court shall decide the question of parental authority over the common minor child". When deciding in which of the parties the exercising of parental authority is to be vested, the court should be guided by the idea of the child's welfare. Sometimes the causes of breakdown indicate the proper decision: habitual alcoholism or prostitution of either parent may be enough to disqualify them. In such a case the hiding of the real causes may be to some purpose: if the spouses agree unanimously to give the child to the disqualified party, they would be helped by hiding the real causes from the court; on the other hand, if they contest the custody of the child, the display of those causes will influence the decision of the court, and therefore hiding them is in the interest of the party whom they bring into disrepute.

However, situations in which the causes of breakdown are the only circumstance indicating to whom the custody of the child should be entrusted, are uncommon: there are, usually, numerous factors which, having impact on the physical and emotional development of the child, should influence the decision of the court. Professor Gellhorn, quoting the opinion of a person of broad experience in dealing with delinquent and neglected children, given in a particular case, mentions, among other factors, "the age of the parents, their economic status, their religious affiliations, the length of their acquaintance before marriage..., the kind of disputes about visitation which occurred since the parties had separated, the adequacy of the care the child had been receiving, the relationship between the father and those with whom he lives, the basis on which he lives with them..., the ages of those persons, whether or not they have, or have had, any children, whether the woman" living in the father's household "had ever taken care of children, the extent of contact between the woman and the child, the amount of time the father had actually spent with the child while she was in the custody of the mother, and the circumstances under which he had spent time with the child". Professor Gellhorn does, moreover, emphasize the necessity of considering "such matters as the affection of the child for the various adults, the real reasons why the contending adults sought custody, and their capacity to build mature relationships despite the strain of marriage breakup" [30]. It is clear that those traits and behaviour of either spouse which have contributed to the occurrence of the marital failure, should often be taken into account also, but rarely as the only or even the most important factor [31].

Nevertheless, the parties in a divorce suit are inclined to treat the faults of their partners as if they were the only factor of import, and

[30] W. Gellhorn, *op. cit.*, p. 313, 315.

[31] Cf. Decree of the Polish Supreme Court of 30 November, 1954, 2 CR 1229/54.

this inclination results in the tendency to hide the real and present the sham causes of breakdown. This tendency clearly appears in the suits in which the parties contest the custody of the child; each party believes that the proper way to prove his own parental abilities is the defamation of the other spouse, and in particular the making known of those of his faults which have caused the marital failure; in consequence the contest for the custody of the child is usually marked by firm disagreement as to who is guilty of the breakdown. This was actually the case in the suits attended: in 18 of them the parties contested the custody of the child, and mutual faultfinding appeared in all the 18; and in 8 of these 18 cases the parties explicitly told the court that they contested the question of guilt in order to succeed in contest for the child.

The hiding of the real causes and symptoms of breakdown, and the producing of bogus ones to attain the procedural goals mentioned above was clearly brought to light in the suits attended, as well as in interviews. It came out mainly in those trials where the parties contested: contradictory statements concerning causes and symptoms indicated an attempt to deceive the court. It is, of course, true that contradictory statements do not necessarily mean that one of the parties is lying: they may be an effect of divergent views or conjectures. This may be the case, in particular, if the wife believes her husband has committed adultery which he denies; if the wife gives her lack of strength, and the husband her laziness as the reason for her neglect of the household; if one of them considers their marriage as maladjusted, and the other as quite happy. However, where the contradictory statements concern objective facts with which the parties involved are undoubtedly well acquainted, it is clear that one of the spouses is deceiving the court. Various lies came to light in this way in the course of the trials attended. The most frequent subject giving rise to such contradictions was whether the husband drank and had been cruel to the wife: had beaten, kicked, insulted her, threatened her with murder; and whether he behaved in a like manner to other persons, in particular the wife's mother and the children. In 15 cases contradictory statements were made concerning when discontinuance of cohabitation had started; here sometimes the defendant wife protested that the parties had lived together up to the last moment, and the husband affirmed that separation had continued for years. In other cases the parties contested whether the husband had supported the family, whether he had compelled the wife to unnatural sexual intercourse, whether the wife had visited the ill husband in hospital, whether she had been expelled from the home or had deserted it of her own will, whether the marriage had been contracted under duress, whether the wife had told the husband about her past. Instances could be multiplied: altogether in 75 of the 153 suits attended it was apparent that for reasons of procedural tactics one of the parties was deceiving the court.

These were mainly the trials in which the parties aimed at divergent goals. The situation differs if the spouses, unanimously agreed on a common purpose, cooperate to deceive the court: in such cases the lies do not come out in court unless the parties cooperate inefficiently or, under the influence of emotion, forget the common purpose and start quarrelling. On the other hand, the lies of the parties aiming at a common goal came out in some interviews with divorcees. One of them said that, in fact, his marriage had not been as happy as the parties had initially expected, but they were "quite a harmonious couple", and, in the event of dismissal of the petition for divorce, "it would have worked reasonably well"; therefore, for want of visible causes and symptoms of breakdown, the barrister "asked us to set forth any facts which could serve as reasons for divorce, but no such facts had occurred. He then wrote the petition in my wife's name, which I had asked him to do, and thought out several charges. I did not agree, and he eventually suggested as a reason the complete breakup of marriage because of the lack of children" (D-22). One of the women interviewed had told the court that she wished to marry again which was untrue, in order "to speed up the case" (D-79); another one explained: to obtain divorce "I had to assure the court that I intended to enter into a new marriage union; however it wasn't true" (DA-7). And another subject confessed: "Since the court had refused to grant us a divorce once, the barrister... decided to deal with the matter firmly and wrote untrue things in the petition, so that even my wife asked him not to exaggerate so much, but I didn't mind, I only wanted to get it all over as soon as possible" (D-9). Similar situations were reported in further interviews; and it seems that, in reality, those situations were more frequent than suggested by the answers of divorced persons, for not all the divorcees who had deceived the court would be inclined to confess it in the interview.

4. THE CONTESTED AND UNCONTESTED TRIAL

The above considerations indicate that the way the parties deceive the court depends on whether they aim at the same or different goals. Hence the necessity of dividing all divorce suits into two groups. The first group consists of cases where contest arose in the course of the suit, regarding any of the above mentioned factors: divorce, guilt, or custody of the child. The second consists of the cases where the parties had agreed on all those points, and, consequently, there was no contest. The suits in the first group we will call contested, those belonging to the second – uncontested cases.

In the sample of 153 trials attended there were 80 contested and 71 uncontested. The remaining 2 could not be included in either group: the spouses had been reconciled at the very beginning of the trial, which in one case resulted in withdrawal of the petition, in the other in permanent suspension of proceedings; therefore neither contest nor agreement as to the procedural goals appeared. The contested trials are not a homogeneous group: they differ as to permanency and intensity of contest. In 10 of the 80 contested trials the proceedings had not been concluded by the end of my observation, in 70 – the proceedings were brought to a conclusion. In 58 of those 70 the contest continued till the conclusion. In the remaining 12 the contest died out during the trial: the parties came to an agreement as to the procedural goals. In coming to the agreement they were guided by various motives: the emergence of a new partner, the hopelessness of contest, tiredness. These reasons came out clearly in court and in interviews: the only reason for which I eventually agreed to divorce was that "my present husband had appeared" (D-86); "I came to the conclusion that we should never become reconciled. I therefore agree to divorce" (T-117); my husband "had no way out, he was afraid of witnesses, had realised he wouldn't succeed, and therefore finally gave up, consenting on the question of guilt" (D-39); "I have no strength to continue the proceedings" (T-106); "I must put an end to it, I am in an awful state of nerves and don't sleep all the night before every appearance in court" (T-100); "I am going to agree to a compromise, because I am completely worn out" (T-115) – these last remarks, heard in the corridor of the court, are the more easily understood if one takes into account the fact that the contested trials attended lasted, on the average, 17.7 months, 16 of them continuing over 2 years, and the longest – 4.5 years; and that the contest is usually very acute. Only in 4 of the contested cases attended did no real struggle appear: these were the curatorial suits, where the curator, having represented the defendant of unknown residence, was in duty bound to request dismissal of the petition, but his request was not followed by any genuine defence of the marriage union. All the above mentioned figures are shown in Table 4.

TABLE 4

Classification of the Trials Attended

Kind of trial		Number of trials
contested trials	not concluded	10
	contested till conclusion	58 (in this 4 curatorial suits)
	contest died out during the trial	12
uncontested trials		71
reconciliation at the beginning of the trial		2
	TOTAL	153

5. LEARNING OF BREAKDOWN IN CONTESTED TRIALS

5.1. In contested cases the court is usually able to learn the most important causes and symptoms of breakdown known to the spouses themselves, or at least enough of them to appraise the degree and permanency of marital failure. This is due, first, to the testimony of the parties themselves. It is true that the information furnished by the parties is not always reliable: contradictions emerged showing that one of the parties was lying in 75 of the trials attended, as I mentioned above. However, lying did not occur in all the contested cases; moreover, it usually concerned certain particular factors and not all the causes and symptoms of breakdown; and, furthermore, the lie of one spouse was frequently cleared away by truthfulness on the part of the other.

What data indicate that a spouse in a contested case is telling the truth? It is mainly his behaviour, and, in particular, the way in which his testimony is given: the coherence of his statements and their accordance with the whole situation emerging in the course of the trial; also his partner's way of testifying, especially if lies and inconsistencies are shown up in the partner's statements. Sometimes the spouse's sincerity is striking: it may be indicated by the emotions he displays, his reactions to the words of his partner, sometimes even by his naiveté or stupidity if they are such that he is unable to deceive the court. In 9 of the 80 contested trials contained in my sample it was the appearance or behaviour of the accused spouse that indicated, with high degree of probability, the existence of at least some of the alleged causes or symptoms of breakdown. For instance, the husband's behaviour in the courtroom implied that he was, as stated by his wife, a psychopath; the apparent pregnancy of a wife, who had deserted her husband years before, implied her sexual relations out of marriage; the tipsiness of the husband in the court and his slovenly appearance indicated that he was probably a drunkard; the wife's exceptional aggressiveness made her husband's complaints as to her difficult character more credible. In 16 contested cases there was another evidence of truthfulness: the spouse disclosed the circumstances indicating the causes and symptoms of breakdown, which, from the procedural point of view, were contrary to his interests; it is clear that one does not think up such circumstances. Thus, e.g., when requesting the court to dismiss the petition because allegedly no breakdown existed, the defendant wife confessed that "there were controversies, quarrels and a hell of life at home, and every return home... resulted in suffering" (T-1). In case T-105 the defendant husband, whose morbid meanness had been the main factor contributing to the breakdown of marriage, told the court, despite his request for dismissal, that though he had been reasonably well off, he had brought his wife and child to starvation. "I beat my wife twice" stated the plaintiff whose wife, aiming at dismissal, charged him with the whole guilt of the breakdown (T-111); and in another case the plaintiff husband admitted that he had had intercourse with his wife "till the last moment" (T-58). Lastly – another circumstance making deceit rather unlikely: in 31 of the 80 contested cases the spouse told the court about the facts which were visibly disagreeable or even shaming to himself. "The doctor has found I am suffering from venereal disease; I had been infected before marriage, by my husband" said the wife in case T-57. In the case T-83 the parties confirmed, reluctantly and with apparent shame, the words of a witness: the plaintiff "had long wanted to dissolve the marriage union, because she was told... that, before marriage, her husband had cohabited with her mother". In other cases the spouses told the court about their own unfaithfulness, concubinage, abortions, illegitimate children and pregnancies, imprisonment for maltreating of wife and children, alcoholism and anti-alcoholic treatment.

The sincerity with which the parties reveal to the court facts which it would be in their interests to hide, as well as disagreeable or even shaming facts, is sometimes an outcome of simple honesty. Frequently, however, it results from another factor: the occurrence of some causes and symptoms of breakdown can easily be provable. This is the case, for instance, with pregnancy, birth of an illegitimate child, anti-alcoholic treatment, imprisonment: to prove them it is enough to present a birth certificate, medical certificate or sentence of the criminal court. Even if the partner of the spouse whose guilt these circumstances prove does not present the above evidence, to prove them is usually so easy that the guilty spouse cannot but confess them frankly.

As it follows from what has been said above, in a contested case it is not only the appearance and behaviour of the parties which indicate truth and falsehood; there are also the other means, mainly the testimony of witnesses and documents, which enable the court to ascertain whether the statements of the parties as to the causes and symptoms of breakdown are true. As a matter of fact, the value of the evidence given by witnesses is limited: it is commonly known how frequently their testimony is far from being true because of forgetfulness, fantasy or lying. However, there is a certain proportion of witnesses – it would be difficult to gauge what proportion – on whose statements one can safely rely. Here again various data indicate whether a witness is telling the truth. Some of them are similar to those which make it possible to judge of the truthfulness of the parties' testimony: the coherence of statements, their accordance with the whole situation, sometimes also emotions displayed by the witness. Relation between the witness and the parties is another important indication. Sometimes witnesses reveal facts disagreeable to themselves, which makes their testimony more trustworthy. There also appear the other data indicating their truthfulness, in particular their unanimity, the more so if they are numerous: if 18 witnesses – all of whom had been called in the case – state that the plaintiff wife had been on intimate terms with her husband's colleague, that "she had constantly met him", that "they had left together for week-ends" and "he had visited her at home in the absence of the husband" (T-5), the number of witnesses and their unanimity indicate that this was probably the case.

Documentary evidence is generally believed to be particularly trustworthy: if the documents are authentic, their contents do not depend upon anybody's memory or veracity. Hence the high value of documents in a divorce suit. In the contested suits in my sample their number was considerable. In 16 cases criminal court sentences or punitory decisions of executive bodies were presented; they indicated the committing of various kinds of offences: cruelty to the other spouse and children, offences committed under the influence of alcohol, thefts, malversations. In 11 cases medical certificates made evident bodily injuries resulting from the beating of wives, and disorders such as venereal and mental diseases which caused or indicated marital failure; in 13 there were various police certificates or criminal court records; 5 wives presented documents testifying that their husbands had had anti-alcoholic treatment; in 9 cases the unfaithfulness of the parties was indicated by letters and photographs. The birth certificates proved considerable difference of age between the parties, which, in their opinion, had influenced the growth of breakdown. The birth certificates of illegitimate children proved unfaithfulness, and certificates of the husband's residence with another woman indicated permanent separation and concubinage. There were also other kinds of documents: petition from neighbours asking the housing authorities to remove the wife, a drunkard and a brawler, from the lodgings of the parties; copies of groundless mutual delations addressed to the public prosecutor; reports of curators of minors which sometimes, by way of presenting the child's situation, threw light on the causes and symptoms of breakdown. In 1 of the 4 curatorial suits a certificate from a psychiatric hospital stating the incurable insanity of the spouse was presented, and in the remaining 3, certificates indicating that the defendant's address had long been unknown. In all, in 55 of the 80 contested cases contained in my sample, documents were presented indicating various factors and symptoms of marital failure. It is clear that they confirm the veracity of statements of the party who presents them; on the other hand, if the other spouse contradicts those statements, the documents prove that he is lying: for, what is the value of the husband's assertions that he neither drank alcohol nor maltreated his wife, if the wife presents a certificate of anti-alcoholic treatment or a sentence of the criminal court convicting him for maltreatment?

5.2. Besides the causes and symptoms of breakdown displayed by the spouses themselves and by witnesses and documents, there is, in a considerable number of contested cases, another factor which the court can easily state. This is the atmosphere of contest itself indicating frustration and wrong caused by breakdown of marriage, want of affection between the spouses, fear, disgust, the wish to humiliate the other party, and, above all, hatred. It was hatred which emerged with particular clarity: it was indicated by mutual fault-finding and outbreaks of anger, and the parties confessed it to each other in the courtroom. Let me present a characteristic instance. According to the words of the plaintiff wife, her husband, lazy, neurasthenic and crude, of a quarrelsome temper, obsessively suspected her of adultery. We left each other, because "he called me... a whore..., he constantly dogs my steps, asks the children whether anybody is visiting me, spies upon me in my job..., attacks me in the street..., when he saw me in a café he called me a strumpet... He demoralizes the children by mixing them up in our affairs". Concluding, she says violently: "this gentleman still hopes for reconciliation, but I assure the Court that, even in the event of dismissal, the Court cannot compel me to cohabit with him, I will never return to him nor forget his insults, I despise him". This declaration was followed by his words: "I had proposed to her to reconcile, but she refused, saying: 'I loathe you, you are a reptile..., I have not paid alimony allowances for the children for several months, because my wife has told me that they were not mine... Now I don't believe we could ever become reconciled, because one can live together only with a human being...; I don't want to join her again" (T-84). Similar feelings were expressed by the parties in many other cases: "I have been afraid of him, he is an accomplished villain, I hate him and won't become reconciled" (T-28); "if I had to choose imprisonment or living together with my wife, I would prefer to be imprisoned" (T-105). These declarations were accompanied by mutual fault-finding, and twice the number of the accusations presented was so large that the party came to the court with a note-book in which they were put down, in order not to forget any grudge. Emotions, anger, bitterness, were revealed by crying, shouting, laughing – in answer to the lies of the other spouse, expression of face, the swelling of veins on the forehead, nervous gestures, the trembling of the voice and hands. There were quarrels and mutual insults, and only energetic admonition on the part of the court restored order. In all – the atmosphere of 24 of the 80 contested trials revealed hatred between the parties. In a further 10 the atmosphere did not show hatred, but still, the display of frustration and wrong caused by conflict between the parties indicated complete failure of the marriage. So in case T-113 the wife revealed, in a detailed testimony, the history of her marriage with a thief and drunkard, and also made known those causes of conflict of which he had not been guilty: her strict education in childhood and the sexual maladjustment of the parties; then she said with sorrow, but without anger: "I can forgive him adulteries and poverty, but not humiliations and shame". In a curatorial suit T-99 the plaintiff wife, moved to such a degree she was hardly able to speak, told the court how her husband, going about as a would-be travelling salesman, had cheated people: "I was silly, naive, and didn't know that he committed several abuses", mainly "to the detriment of women with whom he had cohabited; then they came to me and requested money". He had disappeared and been wanted by the police for two years. "I am, as a result of all that, suffering from heart and nervous disease". Indifference toward the partner's pains and pleas for sympathy indicated want of affection; the wife was not moved by the tears of her husband who said: "I wished for reconciliation, but my wife did not... I am against divorce..., because I love her... I am an orphan, without anyone else" (T-26). Sometimes the parties displayed fear or disgust: "I am afraid of my husband" (T-85), "I left my wife because I loathed her" (T-137). In almost all the contested cases the judge asked the parties whether there was any chance of reconciliation. The majority of denials was decided: "I really cannot stand him any more, he is unfit for a common life" (T-145), "I would prefer to be hanged than become reconciled" (T-44), "I would rather be dead" (T-111).

5.3. When pronouncing divorce in a contested case, the court bases its decision on all the above mentioned forms of evidence: the behaviour, statements and appearance of the parties and witnesses, the documents and atmosphere of the trial. Taking all this into account, the court learns what the causes and symptoms of marital failure are, and, if they are convincing enough, concludes that complete and permanent breakdown of marriage has occurred. This conclusion is not, however, equally justified in various divorce decrees. For, the quantity and trustworthiness of the means employed to prove the causes and symptoms of breakdown vary from case to case. Moreover, the causes and symptoms presented in various suits are not equally convincing as to the completeness and permanency of breakdown; thus, even if the facts revealed in the court undoubtedly prove the occurrence of the causes and symptoms maintained by the party, it does not necessarily mean the breakdown is indeed complete and permanent. Consequently, the conclusion that a marriage has become a complete failure may be far more justified in some decrees than in others. The greater the degree of certainty in the practice of the courts, the better the above mentioned legislative goal is achieved: the limiting of divorce to the instances where the marriage has completely and permanently broken down. Hence the necessity of measuring to what extent this conclusion is justified in the practice of Polish courts.

To measure the degree, all the contested cases which finally resulted in the pronouncement of divorce should be classified. The classification will be arranged in a three-grade scale. The first group will contain the suits where the completeness and permanency of breakdown was proved in the court with a probability amounting almost to certainty. The following are the instances. In case T-31 the plaintiff wife had remained for 20 years in concubinage, and the defendant, disabled because of incurable insanity, had lived in a closed psychiatric hospital, whose certificate was submitted to the court; a guardian, male-nurse of the hospital, represented him in the suit. In case T-142 the separation had lasted for 30, the husband's concubinage for 29 years, and his son, born in concubinage, was of age. In another case there appeared several factors contributing to the breakdown. The husband, who, in 1959, had married the plaintiff wife, older than himself, for pecuniary reasons, beat, kicked, strangled and maltreated her, so that she once got a clot of blood in the mouth; another time he hit her head against the wall and threatened her with a knife: all these facts were confirmed by numerous witnesses and a sentence of the criminal court convicting him of maltreating her. Moreover, he got to know, after marriage, that she had been, during the war, placed in a brothel for German soldiers. This information, as well as his cruelty, resulted in mutual hatred, clearly displayed in the courtroom (T-77). Lastly, in case T-106, the defendant wife had been afflicted with serious nervous troubles, stimulated by the family conflict. She had an affair with a blackmailer who forced her to rob her husband and mother-in-law to prevent him revealing her infidelity, which was subsequently confirmed in another suit going on before the criminal court, in the correspondence submitted by the plaintiff, and in testimony of witnesses. This situation resulted in her attempted suicide and three periods in a psychiatric hospital. The divorce suit lasted for about 3 years, and the parties, defaming each other, displayed not only complete lack of affection, but also extreme ruthlessness.

In none of the suits here described can the assertion of the court as to the completeness and permanency of breakdown be regarded as certain. Even seemingly convincing evidence may prove misleading: documents may be falsified, or the decree of the court gained by means of abuse. Moreover, the assumption of permanency is always based upon prediction of the future relations between the parties, and this kind of prognosis can never be regarded as certain [32]. Therefore in all these

[32] See on this M. Rheinstein, "The Law of Divorce and the Problem of Marriage Stability", *Vanderbilt Law Review*, vol. IX (1956), p. 638.

and like suits there appears only a probability, not certainty of completeness and permanency of marital failure; however, the degree of probability is here so high that it should be regarded as amounting almost to certainty.

The second group will be composed of the trials where the degree of probability, though not equalling that of the first, is still very high. The following are a few instances. In case T-56 the plaintiff, after 32 years of married life in which two children had been born and brought up, entered into concubinage with a woman 25 years younger than himself, and persistently fought for divorce. The previous petition, filed in 1957, had been dismissed by the court of the first instance because of his unilateral guilt, and his ensuing appeal was ineffective. His subsequent request for renewal of proceedings [33] had been ignored by the court, and the ignoring decision appealed against, also without result. The second suit, filed in 1961, was contained in the sample attended. The plaintiff revealed an urgent desire to obtain a divorce in order to marry the concubine, and he demanded, in particular, that the case should be withdrawn from the hands of the judge who had been conducting it, in his opinion, too slowly; in the courtroom he imputed to his wife adultery, a quarrelsome temper, inadequate care of children. Irrespective of whether these charges were justified, the atmosphere of the suit, as well as the persistency with which the plaintiff aimed at dissolution of the marriage in the previous and the attended suit, indicated the completeness and permanency of breakdown with a very high degree of probability. This degree was here, however, lower than in the suits contained in the former group: here the concubinage amounted to 6 years and the parties had cohabited for 32 years, and moreover, the difference of age between the plaintiff and the concubine was great; therefore some chance of his return to the wife and children could not be excluded, especially in case of the concubine's deserting him. In another case frequent marital quarrels were proved, as well as the husband's alcoholism, conflict between his family and the defendant wife, a 4-year separation of the parties. Moreover, the plaintiff imputed to the wife relations with several men, as well as informing during the war which, in his opinion, had resulted in his being put into a concentration camp. She initially did not consent to divorce, aiming at recon-

[33] According to the norms contained in the Code of Civil Procedure, a finally concluded trial can be renewed in some exceptional cases, in particular if new important facts come to light or means of obtaining evidence are used which had not been available in the course of the trial.

ciliation. However, having heard those charges, she said that, after his statement, she did not see any possibility of becoming reconciled; in particular "in view of him accusing me of informing... and continuous infidelity... I am unable to return to the common life" (T-117).

The suits where there also appeared a probability of completeness and permanency of breakdown, but not with such clarity, should be included in the last group. Only one case can be given as an instance here, because only one appeared in the sample observed. At the conciliatory session the plaintiff refused to become reconciled with the wife who, in his opinion, had been unfaithful to him; she answered she would not consent to divorce, since the breakdown of the marriage was the outcome of his, not her, unfaithfulness. The plaintiff, subsequently examined in another court [34], insisted that he had married her because of her alleged pregnancy, and that after getting married she confessed the pregnancy had only been a lie. The parties, who had lived in the country, had only had a civil wedding, without the subsequent religious ceremony [35]. After the marriage they never lived under the same roof, and their intercourse lasted, according to the plaintiff, for 3 months only. His wife had never cared for him, took his money to buy alcohol, had relations with other men. This testimony was also confirmed in another court by his sister and neighbour. The defendant, despite threefold summons, did not appear in the court, and the court eventually pronounced divorce without having examined her; she did not appeal (T-15). If the plaintiff's information is regarded as true, a high degree of probability of complete and permanent breakdown may well be assumed in this case. This information was, however, furnished by the plaintiff only, and supported by 2 witnesses connected with him; moreover, it was not presented in the court which pronounced divorce, and therefore that court could not learn the atmosphere of the trial. Hence the above conclusion that the completeness and permanency of the breakdown were here proved with a considerable degree of probability.

5.4. So much for criteria of classification of contested trials which finally resulted in divorce. There remains to reckon how many should

[34] A party who lives in a distant place can be, under the Polish procedure, examined in the court of the district in which he is resident; then this court sends the divorce court the minutes of testimony.

[35] Which, because of the strong religious attachment of those who live in the rural areas, was rather unusual and could have indicated want of serious intent of living together.

be included in each group. In 58 of the 80 contested trials attended a final divorce decree was issued. In 45 of them the probability of completeness and permanency of breakdown amounted almost to certainty. In a further 12 a very high degree of probability was evident. In 1 case the degree was considerable. There was no suit in the sample in which at least a considerable degree of probability did not exist.

These figures indicate that the Cracow Court, in pronouncing divorce, states in almost every case the completeness and permanency of breakdown with a high degree of probability. This means that the legislative goal under consideration is achieved, in contested cases, to a great extent.

6. LEARNING OF BREAKDOWN IN UNCONTESTED TRIALS

6.1. Poverty of statistical data makes it impossible to ascertain what proportion of all the divorce trials in Poland is made up of uncontested suits; this proportion is, however, undoubtedly remarkable. In the sample attended there were 71 uncontested cases. According to the above conjectures, it is mainly these which give rise to the danger of divorce without complete and permanent marital failure. For, aiming at unanimous procedural goals, in particular at obtaining divorce, the spouses present sham causes and symptoms of breakdown either for want of real ones or in the event that giving a truthful account is for any reason inconvenient to themselves. In effect they make it impossible for the court to check the occurrence, degree and durability of breakdown; and the lack of this check results in the dissolution of working marriages.

Are these conjectures true? The interviews of divorcees indicate that, at least to some degree, they are: over a dozen subjects confessed that they had concealed, in an uncontested case, various important facts, or presented sham ones. These concealments were not all of equal import. They mostly consisted in the hiding of some of the causes and symptoms of breakdown: "I did not reveal all the causes because it was not necessary, those displayed were quite enough to obtain divorce" (D-62); I wanted to avoid "washing our dirty linen in public", and therefore didn't reveal my wife's abortion in court, in spite of the fact that "it had definitely estranged me from her" (D-84); sexual maladjustment was admitted, but the parties concealed the husband's faithlessness and quarrels which "eventually resulted in separation" (D-25). In those and like cases at least some of the causes and symptoms were made known to the court. Some subjects went further and, having concealed all the real elements of conflict, used, to explain its appearance, the vague concept of "incompatibility of characters". The suits attended and interviews given by judges and barristers indicate that the effectiveness of this explanation depends upon the attitude of the judge. The majority of judges, finding it insufficient, ask for more detailed information. Some of them, however, content themselves with generalities: "for the advancement of science I am telling the complete truth which I didn't want to reveal in the court" said a subject who, in the courtroom, gave incompatibility of characters as the reason of breakdown, and in the interview made known in detail its real causes and symptoms (D-24). Another subject, having hidden everything essential, presented the court with a rather unimportant element of conflict as the main cause of marital failure (D-121). From there it is only a step to hiding all the real causes and symptoms and presenting only the sham before the court: "we agreed that the husband would, with the barrister's aid, formulate the petition, offering any causes of breakdown" (D-74); the wife, because of her profession, asked that the real causes of breakdown should not be revealed in the course of the suit, "and I agreed to anything to put an end to it all; the barrister told me what he would say to the court, and I didn't oppose" (D-12).

The concealing of the truth and presenting of sham circumstances made known by the subjects interviewed does not necessarily imply lack of complete and permanent breakdown of marriage: the majority of those subjects who confessed the concealments revealed in the interviews causes and symptoms which inclined one to assume that the marriage had, indeed, become a complete failure. Nevertheless, two of them rèvealed in the interviews the absence, and the third the likelihood of absence, of irretrievable marital failure. In case D-71 the divorced wife said that, as result of presenting sham circumstances to the court, she had obtained a "completely fictitious divorce": her marriage had always been very happy, and divorce was wanted by her husband to get an immigration visa to a foreign country; he subsequently left for that country and she was preparing herself for departure in order to join him abroad. In case D-100 the parties had become reconciled a few months after divorce; they resumed cohabitation and wrote the court a letter asking for "annulment of divorce", which, of course, was not a triable issue. The defendant husband said in the interview that he had not wanted a divorce, "but male pride did not allow opposing and retaining my wife by force": they now live together and intend to re-marry. Lastly, in the above mentioned case D-22, the degree of breakdown seemed to be inconsiderable: according to the husband's words "we constituted quite a harmonious couple...; there were no conflicts. Remoteness simply grew between us, and we came to the conclusion that we were becoming a marriage without affection. This type of relationship did not coincide with our wishes, and we agreed that we should part and wait for a new affection... The barrister asked us to present any facts which could be given as reasons for divorce" but, since none had occurred, he suggested childlessness as the cause of breakdown. In the event of dismissal the marriage "would have worked reasonably well", and "would not have been worse than 60 per cent of those existing, but in our opinion" it did not merit continuation. Like situations have also been reported by some of the barristers interviewed. In their practice there had occurred uncontested cases where the parties, despite absence of breakdown, had claimed and obtained divorce in order to get a better flat, to escape the liability for the other spouse's debts, to retain a professional position endangered by an offence committed by the other spouse. Furthermore, there were cases where the bringing of the suit had been an outcome of simple rashness, a temporary whim or an unimportant quarrel, and immaturity or pride had prevented the plaintiff from withdrawing the petition and the defendant from revealing the insignificance of the conflict.

What is the scope of the problem? What proportion of uncontested cases results in pronouncement of divorce without complete and permanent breakdown? To interview divorcees is not the proper way to find the answer: for, the obtaining of such a divorce is the result of deceit, and it is uncertain whether all those who deceived the court are inclined to admit it in an interview. The proper way of finding the answer is, as in the contested cases, observation in the courtroom.

6.2. In an uncontested trial also the court may appraise the degree and durability of breakdown only by means of learning its causes and symptoms. These can be learned from the data similar to those which make it possible to learn of them in contested cases. In the first place the testimony of each spouse should be mentioned: its truth is indicated, as in the contested suit, by its coherence, accordance with the whole of the situation emerging, the way the other spouse testifies. The sincerity of the party here also is shown by his emotions. In 38 of the 71 uncontested trials attended it was indicated by the fact that the party revealed circumstances the mentioning of which was disagreeable or even embarrassing for himself: there appeared, as in the contested cases, venereal disease, alcoholism and brutality, faithlessness and illegitimate children, abortions, imprisonment, etc. The disclosure of circumstances which, from the point of view of procedural tactics, should have been concealed, appeared twice, indicating the particular truthfulness of the party: in one case the plaintiff wife confessed that she had cohabited with the defendant until the suit started, and in another, where prolonged separation and concubinage of the plaintiff husband were presented as cause and symptom of breakdown, he confessed that there had been a long break in the separation between the parties because of his being on bad terms with the concubine. The witnesses played a very limited role: the procedural provisions enable the court to disregard their testimony in uncontested cases, and, in the majority of the courts under investigation, though not in all, witnesses are examined only in exceptional cases. On the other hand documents are frequently used as evidence in all those courts. Thus, in 19 of the 71 uncontested trials attended, documents had been put before the court to confirm assertions of the parties as to the causes and symptoms of breakdown: among them again were criminal decrees, police certificates, letters, photographs, birth certificates of illegitimate children, reports of curators of minors or social welfare officers, court records, etc. Lastly, the atmosphere of the suit indicated, in uncontested cases also, that the marriage had irretrievably broken down. Here too, there appeared hatred, frustation and wrong caused by breakdown of marriage, fear, disgust, the will to humiliate the other party. Hatred appeared here 4 times; want of affection, frustration and moral pain indicating complete marital failure appeared in 18 of the 71 suits attended. Thus, in case T-25, the defendant wife said, crying: "he makes me miserable, abases me, writes awful letters, calls me a streetwalker...; it was due to him that I am suffering from heart disease...; he always says he must have a woman who will give him everything: home, lodgings...; he demanded that I provide him with a lodging in a fortnight [36], and said he would desert me unless I did...; he never paid anything for the child's maintenance...; he hates the child...; I have no affection for him, only hatred". In another case the marriage had been contracted in 1945, and in 1953 the plaintiff, having left the wife and child without saying good-bye, entered into concubinage, and, subsequently, into a church marriage

[36] Which, because of housing difficulties in Poland, was an impracticable demand.

union with the concubine [37]; a child was born in concubinage. The wife said: "it is very painful for me to speak about it; I loved my husband so much, I sacrificed myself for him, the front still existed, it was during the war, he was hungry and I endangered my life to bring him food. He needed me until he received a diploma, then I became unnecessary and he left me in my absence, without warning... He subsequently was sentenced for non-payment of alimony for the child". Our son "has heart trouble, is so weak and poor, has difficulties at school; fathers of other children keep in touch with the school, but not his father; it is so painful for him". The above words were accompanied by evident feeling of suffered wrong. The plaintiff, when answering to the judge's question as to the possibility of reconciliation, revealed complete indifference and hard-heartedly aimed at divorce (T-103). Mutual fault-finding appeared in 20 of the 71 uncontested suits, and in some of them the charges were so violently imputed by one and opposed by the other party, that the court closed the sitting in tumult and shouting. Anger and bitterness appeared in behaviour similar to that presented above in the description of contested cases. Answers to the questions of the judges aiming at reconciliation were strongly opposed to it: "I have no affection for my husband" (T-54), "I won't be reconciled, he disgusts me" (T-139), "I couldn't live with him any more" (T-153).

6.3. These observations lead to an unforeseen conclusion. In uncontested cases, where, from the point of view of procedural tactics, any struggle between the parties is unnecessary, one might expect – according to the conjecture of the legal writers mentioned above – that everything would proceed quietly, without display of emotions. However, the collected data indicate that this is not the case. It is true that the most violent emotions emerge less frequently here than in the case of contest: evident hatred was made clear in 4 of the 71 uncontested cases while in those contested it came out in 24 out of 80; nevertheless, in a considerable proportion of the uncontested cases the atmosphere is very strained.

This phenomenon can be partially explained by the fact that sometimes even in case of previous consent as to all the procedural goals of the parties, emotions may prevail, and that the consent may not restrain an upset spouse from outpourings. However, the main factor

[37] Which was allowed till 1959; since 1959 every religious marriage must be preceded by civil marriage.

here is the manner in which consent is usually reached between the parties, i.e. the way the divorce suit becomes an uncontested one.

The reasons for which a proportion of the spouses do not contest divorce or guilt were made known in interviews and in the courtroom. The one to be mentioned first is the wish to obtain divorce in a quiet and easy way, without embitterment, making known personal affairs, calling witnesses: "we both wanted to obtain divorce as soon as possible, and to be free, at last, from all the bother" (D-9), "we were for simplifying the case in order to avoid disclosing of various intimate details" (D-12), "I didn't want to wash dirty linen in the court and to call witnesses, it was our intimate affair" (D-32) – these were characteristic declarations of divorcees. Sometimes the party agrees to divorce after having found that there is no chance of reconciliation; this happens either before filing the petition, especially if the spouses have for long remained in separation, or in the early stage of the suit: "I initially had not consented to divorce in order not to lose him..., but then I learned in court that his mistress had given birth to a child, what could I have done then?" (D-56), "my husband came to understand that it was a hopeless case...; that I would never return to him" (D-83), "the barrister told me that irrespective of whether I wanted it or not, my husband would get a divorce, and it would be better not to persist" (D-128). Moreover, the party aiming at divorce frequently offers various forms of remuneration for consent: "my husband had promised me... money, I therefore gave my consent..., this was simply selling a divorce" (D-107); "I wanted to obtain the highest price possible..., that was the only moment when my husband was ready, in order to arrange his affairs, to give any sum; he declared he would make an alimony allowance amounting to 1500 zlotys per month [38], and gave, in addition, 120 thousand" (D-104). Many subjects set forth other reasons: ambition, generosity, love, weakness: "male pride prevented me from opposing and retaining my wife by force" (D-100), "my husband's mistress was pregnant and I didn't want to wrong her" (D-101), "my husband said he would not have intercourse with me anyway, because of my state of health, but he would always love me like a sister; he asked me not to tie him since he still needed a woman", I agreed to everything, for "I love him so much" (D-98).

The parties who because of such motives do not engage in contest either for divorce or on the question of guilt, or give up the contest

[38] The average monthly remuneration of working people in Poland being about 2000 zlotys.

initially raised, do not generally create a strained and hostile atmosphere in court. However, besides these motives, another factor also appears in divorce suits which frequently results in foregoing contest: this is persuasion on the part of the court which usually takes place in the initial part of the suit, generally at the conciliatory session; and where this is the reason for consent, consent does not necessarily insure that the course of the trial will be quiet.

The inducing of the parties to consent takes place at the conciliatory sessions tried by some, not by all judges. It had taken place in 17 of the 84 sessions attended. It was, in all the 17 cases, a persuasion to divorce without deciding the question of guilt [39]. In 15 of them the judge aimed at inducing the spouses to give up contesting the question of guilt which had initially emerged; in the remaining 2 he aimed at inducing the defendant to agree to divorce; he probably did not see any chance of reconciliation. In 10 of the 17 cases here mentioned the judge's persuasion immediately resulted in a request by both parties for divorce without deciding the question of guilt. In the remaining 7 the judge persuaded them to give up the contest in the further course of the suit. The intensity of the judicial persuasion varied. The weakest form was a suggestion "possibly without deciding the question of guilt?" (CS-66). The advice directed to a defendant who initially had refused to consent to divorce without deciding the question of guilt, sounded stronger: "do agree, it doesn't matter, and the case will be concluded quickly; don't you want to marry your concubine?" – and when the defendant, after a lengthy hesitation, answered "yes, I do, sometime in future", the judge insisted again: "now you are being sensible, if you wish to marry her, do agree to divorce without deciding the question of guilt". After the proposal had been repeated four times the defendant eventually said "very well then", and the judge dictated to the recorder: "the parties unanimously request that the divorce be decreed without deciding the question of guilt, and the plaintiff decided against the calling of witnesses" (CS-33). It is only a step away from this to presenting to the parties the prospect of a prolonged and burdensome contest: "does the problem of guilt matter so much to you?... If you want, you can contest it, both parties will lose by that, but you probably prefer a quick conclusion..., the contest of the question of guilt will last two or three years, witnesses will be called, there will be a decree, an appeal, we shall send a curator of minors to inquire into the situation of the

[39] On Art. 57 of the Family and Guardianship Code, enabling the court to pronounce divorce without deciding the question of guilt, see above, p. 24.

children, there have been suits which lasted five years" (S-27). In another case, where the defendant wife insisted, despite the judge's suggestion, on imputing the guilt to her husband, the judge said: "with imputing the guilt it will go on for a further three years"; she tried to oppose again, but the judge declared that "nobody's guilt will be pronounced", and she eventually gave up (CS-40). Sometimes the court treats the behaviour of the parties as if it were an agreement to divorce without deciding the question of guilt, in spite of the fact that it is not: in the case CS-42 the defendant wife, asked by the judge whether she would agree, answered "yes", but the whole situation indicated that she felt lost in court and did not understand the question.

This behaviour of the judges was reflected in the interviews of divorcees. In the sample containing 131 divorcees, there were 95 subjects who obtained divorce in an uncontested trial [40]. 30 of those subjects told the interviewer that contest for divorce or on the question of guilt had not arisen in the courtroom: the plaintiff had requested, in the petition, the pronouncing of divorce without deciding the question of guilt or the imputing of guilt to the respondent, and the respondent consented to that request in the first declaration made in the court. On the other hand, the remaining 65 subjects reported that contradictory requests as to divorce or guilt had initially been made by the parties, and that, subsequently, the contest died out in the initial part of the suit, generally at the conciliatory session. Thus, according to the information furnished by the divorcees, in at least [41] 8 of those 65 trials, the advice or even pressure of the judge was the only factor or one of the factors contributing to giving up of contest. The majority of subjects who, under the influence of the judge, had given up contest, did not regret it, though two of them had a grudge against the court: "the judge

[40] These figures indicate that the proportion of uncontested cases among the trials of the subjects interviewed was much higher than among those attended (see above, Table 4). There are two reasons which explain the difference. First, the interviews were drawn only from the trials which had resulted in divorce, while among the ones attended there were also the cases which either resulted in dismissal or, because of their long duration, were not concluded by the end of my inquiry; and dismissed and prolonged cases are usually the contested. Secondly, the higher the intellectual level of the parties, the more frequently there appears the tendency to uncontested divorce suits; and the average level of education of the subjects interviewed was higher than of those whose suits were attended: those interviewed were only the inhabitants of Cracow, while a considerable part of those whose suits were attended lived in small towns and villages of the province.

[41] There may have been more than 8 cases, because some subjects did not remember or were unable to say who had persuaded them to give up the contest.

proposed divorce without deciding the question of guilt, it seemed that he wanted to speed the work" (D-21); in the courtroom "my husband's barrister talked me down... It was the first time I had ever been in court and I didn't know what was going on, I didn't want to agree" to divorce without deciding the question of guilt, but I was helpless, because the judge and barrister "got round" (D-75). The further 3 women interviewed did not maintain that it was the judge who had induced them to divorce without deciding the question of guilt, but they did not know that they could have demanded the court to impute the guilt to their husbands. Lastly, 4 subjects simply did not know that divorce had been pronounced without deciding the question of guilt: they were convinced the court had imputed the guilt to the other spouse, and not having obtained the copy of the decree [42], they never learned their mistake.

Such behaviour on the part of some of the judges, especially if it amounts to pressure, results in depriving the party of his rights, which has been pointed out in the interviews with some from among these judges who never push the parties to give up contesting. Indeed, the party is often interested in imputing guilt to the other spouse. In particular, if divorce has been pronounced without deciding the question of guilt, the duty to pay alimony between the spouses terminates, in principle, in five years from the date of divorce [43]: that is why persuasion to give up contesting the question of guilt may result in depriving the party of the means of maintenance. It is true that the judges who persuade parties to divorce without deciding the question of guilt usually inform the parties, especially those appearing in court without barristers, about that consequence; but they do not inform them in every case. Moreover, the demand to impute guilt to one of the spouses may be justified by other reasons. In interview D-52 the respondent wife deplored the consent she had given to divorce without deciding the question of guilt: she was convinced that "as a woman" she might "sometime find herself in trouble because of the fact that she had obtained a divorce without her husband's guilt being made evident"; and in case T-70 the defendant wife told me, crying, during an interruption in the sitting of the court preceding the pronouncement of decree, that she had been insulted in the petition and could not clear herself of

[42] According to the procedural provisions, the copy of the divorce decree is obtained only at the request of the party.

[43] This is the contents of Art. 60 Para. 3 of the Family and Guardianship Code, which superseded Art. 34 Para. 1 of the previous Family Code.

the charges in the court; when asked by me why she consented to divorce without deciding the question of guilt, she answered: "the judge induced me to it, in order not to hear witnesses".

The motives which incline the judges to behaviour such as that described, despite the rights of the parties, are strong: they are effective in all the courts in my investigations; in particular 18 of the 35 judges interviewed from Warsaw, Lublin and Katowice persuade the parties, if there is no hope of reconciliation, to consent to divorce without deciding the question of guilt: some of them do it only occasionally, others frequently, 6 of them usually, and the persuasion or pressure exercised by them had been confirmed by barristers' information. Some of these motives were made known by the judges: "I usually persuade" to divorce without deciding the question of guilt, "because this makes the conducting of the suit much easier" (J-37), "If I feel that both parties are guilty, I tell them that the marriage should be dissolved in a gentle way" (J-33), I generally emphasize "the value of a civilized divorce" (J-35), I only persuade in exceptional cases, "if the future of a young woman is concerned" (J-20) or "if the woman is threatened with the imputing of guilt" (J-32), "sometimes it is better not to contest the guilt for the welfare of the children" (J-22), "during the trial one should arrange the future relations between the parties in a reasonable way" (J-3). The judges' experience lies behind their words. The parties' consent as to divorce and guilt, indeed, makes their work easier. It limits the evidence needed: some courts (e.g. in Cracow) do not call witnesses in uncontested cases, the others (e.g. in Warsaw) do call them, but very few, and provided that the spouses have common children under age. Moreover, in an uncontested case appeal does not impend; in consequence the judge avoids the necessity of writing the motives for the decree, and the case will never be tried for the second time. The suffering and weariness of those who enter into contest, which constantly appeared in the courtroom and in interviews, indicate the value of the quiet divorce suit. Sometimes the divorced women make known how important it is for them not to be declared guilty: a 22-year-old defendant wife who, at the time of the marriage, hid venereal disease from her husband, asks the judge with evident anxiety, just after pronouncement of the divorce decree: "will it be mentioned in the decree that it is my fault? What will be said there?"; and her anxiety is not calmed until the judge answers: "your fault will not be mentioned in the decree, and nobody will ever be allowed to look into these records" (T-67). The quiet course of the divorce suit is of particular import to the children of the parties, since anger born of contest is not only harmful to the child's situation during the suit, but reduces also the likelihood of the parties cooperating in the upbringing of the child after divorce: "during the trial we didn't even speak with each other" – said the defendant wife in case T-100 – "but after we had decided to give up contest, the relations between us became quiet and correct; now my husband is more concerned with our daughter, he visits her, gives her gifts, shows her more tenderness". Moreover, the tendency of the court to settle the whole of the future relations between parties with their cooperation is an outcome of a more general tendency to treat the divorce court as a mediatory institution, aiming rather at exercising custody and giving assistance than at making arbitrary decisions; this tendency makes itself evident not only in the persuading of the parties to agree to divorce without deciding the question of guilt, but also in the efforts of some judges to bring the parties to unanimous settlements as to other problems, like custody of the child, alimony allowances, partition or leaving of the common lodging, sometimes even payments in favour of the innocent defendant who claims them in return for consent to divorce, of which more will be said below.

The consideration of whether and to what degree all these motives justify the court in persuading parties to give up contesting, would exceed the limits of the present comments, which do not aim at the appraisal of the judges' behaviour. Their only purpose is to make clear, by means of learning motives of the judges, the role played by their behaviour in terminating contest. For, it is that behaviour which explains the unexpected phenomenon described above: the strained atmosphere of the majority of uncontested cases. Where the parties themselves come to an agreement as to the procedural goals because of the wish to obtain divorce in a quiet way, because of affection, weakness or pecuniary settlement, one would expect a quiet atmosphere in the courtroom. However, where the parties initially aim at contest, in particular at contest concerning the imputing the guilt, and give it up under the influence of the persuasion or pressure of the court, it does not imply that no wish exists to fight, take revenge, give vent to anger, hatred, frustration and the feeling of wrong suffered: all these emotions, having found no outlet in contest, come out in the uncontested trial.

6.4. When pronouncing divorce in uncontested cases, the court bases its decision, as in contested suits, on the collected evidence, in particular on the behaviour, declarations and appearance of the parties, on the documents and atmosphere of the trial. Taking them into account the court learns what the causes and symptoms of marital failure are, and in this way concludes that a complete and permanent breakdown of marriage has occurred. This conclusion is here also not equally justified in various divorce decrees: hence the necessity of the classification of uncontested trials. Unlike that of the contested cases, this classification will be arranged according to a four-grade scale. The first group will here again contain the trials where the completeness and permanency of breakdown had been proved in court with a probability amounting almost to certainty, the second – where there had been a very high degree of probability. Both those degrees were measured above on a sufficient number of instances, thus no new instances seem necessary here. The third group will contain the cases where the degree of probability was considerable. There was only one such case among the contested trials. Here this is a larger group, and therefore another example should be given. The plaintiff wife married in 1952, at the age of 17 [44], a 22-year-old student. She did it because she was pregnant, without affection, out of fear of public opinion. They were initially maintained by the parents, and used to spend their time in night-clubs, dancing and drinking. The defendant made scenes of jealousy, beat his wife after he had been drinking; they ceased living together several times and then returned to cohabitation. In 1956 the wife brought a petition for divorce, but then withdrew it after having been reconciled. The trial attended started in 1961. According to the wife's words, her husband "has drunk for 5 years, sometimes he drank for the whole week, when I asked him... where he had been drinking, he answered: 'you whore..., it is not your business'. I once slapped him in the face, and then he beat me, in 1960 he slapped me, in 1956 he beat me severely and therefore I filed a petition for divorce..., then I withdrew it, but his behaviour did not improve..., we ceased cohabitation 8 months ago and a month ago I left his lodgings, I despise him". The husband told the court that the wife "had spent money on dresses and coats, and, as a result, had not enough to live on..., we had arguments because of jealousy..., I was going to places of entertainment without her in order to spite her, all that resulted in quarrels..., blows, my drinking; I don't despise my wife, we ceased cohabitation a month ago, in my opinion we could continue living together provided that we both changed...,

[44] According to the previous and the present family codes, a woman under the age of 18 cannot contract a marriage; however, the guardianship court may, for serious reasons, grant permission to marry to a woman over the age of 16.

but, in view of my wife's attitude, I don't insist on continuance of the marriage".

The last group of the uncontested trials contains those where the probability of completeness and permanency of breakdown did not clearly appear. These are a few instances. In case T-8 the plaintiff wife told the court: "my husband hit me more than once, he had a grudge against me because of my thriftlessness, he was good to the child... When I was pregnant he did not care for me, he laughed when I cried..., we have had a common lodging, now he hopes to get a separate one". The defendant confessed that there had been quarrels and sometimes beatings, but when asked about their reasons, he answered vaguely: "there was no common language, our interests varied..., there were quarrels concerning the child, his feeding and clothes"; neither spouse said anything more. In case T-66, according to the plaintiff husband, "we have not lived together for a year", it is the result of "incompatibility of characters..., we each have our own friends, at the end of 1960 was a serious quarrel, and my wife demanded that I leave home". In her opinion the marriage became a failure "to a large extent because we had lived with my parents..., my husband was on bad terms with them..., I could no longer bear the quarrels and my husband's jealousy because of my affection for them, so I ceased to love him". In case T-75 the only circumstances unanimously disclosed by the parties were mental deficiency and cancer from which their 11-year-old child was suffering; moreover, the plaintiff wife asserted that the husband had been living in concubinage, which he absolutely denied. He said only that their "characters were incompatible", and that "every child borne by my wife has been handicapped", in spite of the fact that neither in the petition nor in the courtroom was the birth of any other children mentioned. When asked by the judge why he wanted divorce, he answered: "I must arrange my personal affairs", and when subsequently asked, whether with another woman, he only said "yes", and did not mention her name nor give any other information. Lastly, in the case T-59, the plaintiff wife said that the breakdown had been caused by "incompatibility of characters, by the fact that the husband didn't like any amusements..., that he wasn't sociable..., which often resulted in disagreements...; he was jealous of me and made frequent scenes... Then he started studying..., his character changed, there was a quarrel..., blows, and since then we have ceased living together". The defendant confirmed these statements, and added only: "I liked amusements... and society, but not those that my wife did".

6.5. So much for the criteria of the classification of uncontested trials. Their distribution is as follows. In 70 of the 71 uncontested trials attended divorce was pronounced. In 29 of them the probability of a complete and permanent breakdown amounted almost to a certainty. In 18 there appeared a very high, in 9 a considerable degree of probability. In 14 the probability of the completeness and permanency of breakdown did not appear clearly. Table 5 shows these figures combined with those drawn from the contested cases.

TABLE 5

The Probability of Completeness and Permanency of Breakdown in the Contested and Uncontested Trials which Resulted in a Final Divorce Decree

Type of trial / Degree of probability of completeness and permanency of breakdown	Group I: probability amounting almost to certainty	Group II: very high degree of probability	Group III: considerable degree of probability	Group IV: no clear probability	TOTALS
contested	45 (77.6 %)	12 (20.7 %)	1 (1.7 %)	—	58 (100 %)
uncontested	29 (41.4 %)	18 25.7 %)	9 (12.9 %)	14 (20.0 %)	70 (100 %)
TOTALS	74 (57.8 %)	30 (23.5 %)	10 (7.8 %)	14 (10.9 %)	128 (100 %)

The above table leads to an interesting conclusion. The cases where divorce was decreed on the ground of the highest degree of the probability of complete and permanent breakdown amounted to 77.6 per cent of the contested trials, and to 41.4 per cent of those uncontested. The proportion of cases where the probability was considerable only amounted to 1.7 and 12.9 per cent respectively. Lastly, among the contested trials there appeared no case without a clear probability, while among those uncontested the proportion amounted to 20 per cent. These data show the difference between finding out the breakdown in the contested and the uncontested trial. In the practice of the Cracow Court this difference is significant [45]. It is, however, not so great as one could have expected when taking into account some of the above

[45] $X^2 = 24.13$ ($P<0.05$, df $= 3$).

mentioned opinions [46]; in the evident majority – viz. in 67.1 per cent – of the uncontested cases, the court does ascertain the completeness and permanency of breakdown with at least very high degree of probability.

7. DIVORCE WITHOUT COMPLETE AND PERMANENT BREAKDOWN OF MARRIAGE

7.1. The final divorce decree was pronounced in 128 of the trials attended, of this number in 58 contested and 70 uncontested suits. The probability of completeness and permanency of breakdown appeared in 114, and did not appear in 14 of them. It seems likely that if there were any instances of divorce without complete and permanent breakdown of marriage, they were probably among those 14 cases, i.e. in 10.9 per cent of all the final divorce decrees of my sample; the figure which I am looking for – the number of divorces without irreparable marital failure – is likely to be contained, as far as the practice of the Cracow Court goes, within those limits.

It is obvious that this figure does not amount to that of divorce decrees pronounced in trials where probability of breakdown did not clearly appear: for, the fact that breakdown did not come out in court does not necessarily imply it had not occurred. In order to approach the actual figure a more detailed analysis of those 14 trials appeared necessary. Hence the interviewing of the persons who had obtained divorce in them. The way the interviews were obtained has been presented above: only that spouse was interviewed who seemed to be more trustworthy or more inclined to furnish information; in want of any conjecture concerning these matters, the woman was interviewed. I did not succeed in contacting 6 divorced couples; 8 subjects – 1 man and 7 women – were interviewed. This way of taking the sample was similar to that used to complete the main sample of divorcees; however, here the content of interviews was completely different: these interviews were intended to ascertain the degree and at least some of the causes and symptoms of breakdown. They were difficult, and the letters which I previously wrote to the subjects interviewed, assuring them that the interview would "not concern any personal matters", were here not fully justified. Each interview started with a colourless and rather unimportant question, preceding two yes-and-no questions. The first

[46] Pp. 33-34.

of them was: "What do you think now: if the court had dismissed the petition for divorce, would you: become reconciled – probably become reconciled – probably not become reconciled – certainly not become reconciled – don't know". The second of them was: "Do you think that then, in your husband's (wife's) opinion, you would become reconciled – probably become reconciled – probably not become reconciled – certainly not become reconciled – don't know". The answers to these questions, and in particular the further disclosures of the subject, were to help in learning the degree of breakdown. Behind the decision to arrange these interviews, there was the belief that the subjects interviewed, and in particular the women, would be inclined to speak extensively on their married life, a belief drawn from the experience gained previously in gathering information from the main sample of divorcees.

This belief appeared justified: it was shown by the content of the information furnished and the atmosphere of interviews. Only one of them did not enable the estimation of the degree of marital failure: in the opinion of the woman interviewed the couple would probably have become reconciled in the event of dismissal, but she had filed the petition at the request of her husband, who had been abroad a long time, and therefore it was rather his information which could have thrown light on the degree of breakdown; however, it was impracticable to interview him because of his absence from Poland. (DA-5)[47]. In 6 further interviews a clear probability of the completeness and permanency of breakdown appeared. Let me present those of them which were taken to throw light upon the trials above exemplified. In interview DA-2, derived from trial T-8, the woman interviewed willingly and minutely described many details of her life with the husband, and in particular wrangles indicating his neurasthenic temper. She had married him out of deep affection, but "the marriage was a failure from the very beginning, there were always quarrels growing more violent with the passage of time". Initially she could not work because of her poor state of health, and she was helped by her parents. The husband reproached her for not working and when she subsequently started working, "he counted every zloty spent by her". On the whole "he was dissatisfied with anything" she did or said. According to her story he had been "an impotent": they had intercourse very rarely, "he didn't need it". This sexual inhibition, hidden by the parties from the court,

[47] The interview derived from trial T-35.

resulted in her nervous exhaustion and made the conflict much more acute. With the birth of the child relations deteriorated even more: there was constant bickering concerning the child, and, soon after her confinement, the husband struck her. She was in such a state that she started neurological treatment, and she filed a petition for divorce "after five years of marriage", since she "could not stand it any longer". She said in the interview that in the event of dismissal they would certainly not have become reconciled: "I would never return to my husband after all I had gone through". In interview DA-4, derived from trial T-66, the defendant woman initially gave vague answers, but subsequently she let herself be drawn into conversation and became sincere. According to the interviewer's report, "she did not reveal everything, but, when analysing some of the information given by her, one would almost certainly conclude that the breakdown had been caused by her affection towards another man and the wish to join him". "I went with my former husband to a barrister known to us", she said, "and we came to the conclusion that my husband should file the petition, since otherwise I would never obtain a divorce. It was unpleasant that the three of us were sitting and thinking up various charges... My husband... said that if I wanted divorce he would help me, although it was very much against his will. She then confessed, having asked for secrecy, that the petition had been completely fictitious. "We put forward my parents who, to tell the truth, had very much liked my husband, since we had to put forward something... In court they put such questions as: did your husband beat you – no, – did you beat your husband? – no, – did your husband drink alcohol? – no, – why do you want a divorce, then?" When asked about the chance of reconciliation, she said with laughter: "I absolutely cannot accept the idea, I remarried some months ago, am very happy, in love, how could I think what would have happened in the event of dismissal?". Lastly, in the interview DA-8, derived from trial T-75, the defendant woman, wasted and resigned, told how her husband, after 10 years of a good married life, lost his fingers in an accident, and, as a result, because he was a locksmith, lost his job; he subsequently made new friends who led him to drink and women. At the same time the son of the parties fell ill with meningitis, the doctors supposed he would die, but he did not, and is mentally deficient; he is, moreover, suffering from cancer of the throat, he cries and moans at nights. In the interviewee's opinion these two events broke her husband. He drank more and more, became acquainted with another woman and eventually went to live with her. In the meantime the wife became pregnant and had to have an abortion, which resulted in complete prostration: "I didn't even want to fight for my husband, I grew indifferent to everything". Now "I meet him sometimes... but he means just nothing to me, I absolutely don't trust him after all he did... He has changed completely, it seems that he does not love our son any more, never visits him, never buys him anything".

In the last of the 8 interviews I am talking about, it appeared that the court had pronounced divorce without complete and permanent breakdown of marriage. It was interview DA-3, derived from trial T-59 [48]. It is true that the conflict, caused mainly by a difficult financial situation and interfering parents, resulted, just before the filing of petition, in the discontinuing of cohabitation, but, in the interviewed woman's opinion, the conflict was not intense and only temporary. She filed the petition for divorce merely to become reconciled. She loved her husband, she was only waiting for any opportunity of reconciliation, and hoped for "a stronger pressure on the part of the judge" which would have helped her to become reconciled "without humiliation". The judge was not active enough, and the husband, "though surprised by my decision as to a divorce, did not propose reconciliation... If we had been induced and persuaded, we would have become reconciled", and if the court had dismissed the petition, it would also have resulted in reconciliation.

7.2. The above presented factual data seem to throw some light on the problem under discussion. Namely, it appeared that in 1 of the 128 divorce decrees, divorce had been pronounced without irreparable marital failure: this amounts to 0.8 per cent. In the further 7 cases – in 6 of which I did not succeed in obtaining an interview, and in 1 case where the interview obtained did not make it possible to appraise the degree of breakdown – it was impossible to ascertain whether complete and permanent breakdown had occurred. Those 7 cases in which no conclusion could be reached and the above mentioned case where the court had decreed divorce without breakdown, amount to 6.2 per cent of all the divorce decrees pronounced in my sample. Hence – conjecture that in the practice of the Cracow Court the proportion of divorces pronounced without complete and permanent breakdown is somewhere between 0.8 and 6.2 per cent; and it seems to be a safe guess that the actual figure is rather near the lower limit. There are two circumstances

[48] See above, p. 66.

which make the guess probable. First, if the majority of the 8 subjects who were interviewed displayed clear probability of breakdown, the probability would possibly have appeared also in the majority of those 6 divorced couples whom I was unable to reach; the more so that the fact of not securing interviews from them was not, for the most part, because of a refusal, but because the parties lived out of Cracow or there were difficulties in finding their correct adresses. Moreover, the experience of 25 Cracow barristers who were interviewed supports this supposition: the mean proportion of final divorce decrees pronounced without complete and permanent breakdown of marriage amounts, according to their information, to 2.0 per cent, the median – to 0.7 per cent; and, as I have already said, they are usually well informed as to the state of the marriages of their clients. Their information seems to be a valuable extension of the data collected in the courtroom and in interviews of divorcees; they represent experience accumulated in the course of approximately 1,860 divorce cases conducted since 1958. The information furnished by 35 barristers from Warsaw, Lublin and Katowice, who had together been charged with the conducting of approximately 2,420 suits, led to a territorial extension of the Cracow data. According to their information, the mean proportion of final divorce decrees pronounced without complete and permanent breakdown amounts to 2.2 per cent, the median – to 1.5 per cent. It is obvious that one should, because of the way my samples have been taken, treat all these figures cautiously; and that the data drawn from the four courts cannot be considered as a solid basis for generalizations. However, in the light of those data it seems to be probable that under the Polish system the proportion of divorces pronounced without irreparable marital failure is low; and that, in consequence, the legislative goal which I am talking about – the limiting of divorce to the events of complete and permanent breakdown of marriage – is being reached to a high degree.

8. SOME MERITS AND DANGERS OF THE ACCEPTED SOLUTION

At the beginning of this chapter I said a word about the expectations which those in favour of the principle of breakdown connect with its introduction. They expect that, due to a more liberal access to divorce than that warranted by the doctrine of matrimonial offence, the above described abuses – divorces obtained on sham grounds, divorce migrations, change of religion, groundless annulment of marriages – would disappear: why deceive the court if every broken marriage can be honestly dissolved? The collected data indicate that in Poland this expectation is far from being fully realised; and it seems to be a safe guess that the same is the case in the other countries which introduce breakdown of marriage as ground for divorce. It is true that under the principle of breakdown the abuses take another and less drastic form than those to be met with under restrictive divorce systems. Nevertheless, there too, the court is frequently deceived by the parties presenting sham and hiding the real causes and symptoms of breakdown. It is true that deception very rarely results in divorce without breakdown; but it also brings "the administration of law into disrepute", to use once again the words above quoted. On this point the introduction of the principle of breakdown has not entirely fulfilled the hopes placed in it. And it seems that it could not: to accomplish them fully a much further liberalization of the divorce law would be needed. Only divorce by consent would exclude collusion in uncontested cases; and in those where one of the spouses wants divorce against the will of his partner, only the system of divorce obtainable on unilateral request, irrespective of the reasons, would fully guard against lies and attempts to hide the truth from the court. Yet, it seems obvious that such a system would go too far.

As I have said above, those who are for the introduction of breakdown as an all-embracing ground for divorce believe that the system which they recommend is the proper way to prevent the dissolution of working marriages and to fix suitable limits to divorce. On the other hand, the adversaries maintain that, due to collusions, its introduction comes near being divorce by consent, which results in divorce pronounced without breakdown, and ultimately in a rapid rise of the divorce rate, endangering the institution of marriage itself.

The collected factual data indicate that these fears are partially grounded: the acceptance of the principle of breakdown often results in collusion as to its causes and symptoms. However, it seems, in the light of the above considerations, that it does not result in frequent divorce without breakdown, obviously subject to the scantiness of the data collected. Thus it should not result in a rapid rise in the divorce rate. Some more general statistics confirm this last conclusion: in Poland the courts pronounced in 1961 – 5.5, in 1962 – 6.0, in 1963 – 6.3, in 1964 – 6.7 divorce decrees per 10,000 of the total population, which is, despite some tendency to increase, a moderate proportion, below the European average.

It certainly would be a mistake to draw too far-reaching conclusions from the above figures, and in particular to maintain that introduction of the principle of breakdown never gives rise to the danger of a rapid growth of resort to divorce. Resort to divorce is an effect not only of legal provisions in force, but also, and mainly, of the whole cultural background of a given community: its socio-economic structure, accepted moral values and sexual patterns, the religious affiliation of its members, etc. That is why the same divorce law may have no serious impact on the divorce rate in one country, and in another give disastrous results. Thus, the above figures indicate only that in the cultural conditions of contemporary Poland the danger does not really exist.

Any detailed analysis of the Polish cultural conditions would obviously exceed the scope of the present considerations. However, two of the social pressures which limit access to divorce seem to be so significant that they deserve mention. The first of them is the economic structure of the country. In spite of a rapid growth of industry in the last two decades, Poland is still to a large extent a rural country; those whose main source of income is farming – farmers and their families – amount to 33.8 per cent of her total population [49]. The rural family, being not only a consumptive, but also a productive economic unit, is bound by economic ties which make it difficult or even impossible to divorce in the event of maladjusted marriages. This is the main reason that in 1960 divorces pronounced in the urban areas, on the average, amounted to 8.7, and in the rural to 1.5 per 10,000 of the total population [50]. For the same reason the process of industrialisation and urbanization of the country contributes to the slow but constant rise of the divorce rate mentioned above. Another social pressure of significance is the influence of the Catholic Church: a survey arranged in 1962 by the Public Opinion Research Centre indicates that approximately 77.8 per cent of Poland's population are Catholic believers, and that the proportion of those opposed to divorce is 3.8 times higher among believers than among those who are indifferent or atheists [51]. One should, however, not exaggerate this influence. The same survey showed that as many as 64.1 per cent of the believers were for the acceptance of divorce, in spite of their religious belief: the cognitive dissonance has been hypothetically explained by a supposition that "the process of laicisation of a community

[49] *Rocznik statystyczny (Statistical Year Book)*, 1965, p. 36.

[50] Data drawn from the Statistical Department of the Ministry of Justice.

[51] A. Podgórecki, *Zjawiska prawne w opinii publicznej (Legal Phenomena in Public Opinion)*, 1964, p. 49.

goes on mainly through changes in the character and functioning of certain institutions, customs, peculiar norms etc., and only later through the modification of general outlook and attitudes" [52]. Anyway, in spite of the above dissonance, religion undoubtedly is an important pressure limiting access to divorce.

Would the acceptance of the principle of breakdown endanger family life in a community with a different cultural background? It is impossible to answer the question in a general manner: one should know the impact of the many factors which change from country to country. However, it seems to be certain that its acceptance has thus far not appeared dangerous in the countries which have introduced it, in spite of the fact that they differ widely from each other. In particular it has not appeared dangerous in countries, like the Soviet Union or Czechoslovakia, where religious affiliation does not play an important role, and where the land holders do not exist or are not a considerable proportion of the population. Neither did any danger appear in the highly developed countries of Western Europe – Switzerland and Western Germany – where, as I have said above, breakdown had been introduced as one of the grounds for divorce. It is true that in all these countries the divorce rate is higher than in Poland: in 1960 it amounted in Czechoslovakia to 11.2, in the Soviet Union to 13.0, in Switzerland to 8.7, in Western Germany to 8.3 divorces per 10,000 of the total population. But this still does not exceed the European average: contrary to conjecture of its adversaries mentioned above, the acceptance of the principle of breakdown did not "undermine and... destroy the concept of life-long marriage" in any of these countries.

[52] A. Podgórecki, *op. cit.*, p. 69.

V

RECONCILIATION

1. GOALS AND CONJECTURES

1.1. The intention to save marriages which are maladjusted, but not to the extent of excluding any hope of effectively mending them, is closely connected with the idea of limiting divorce to the cases of complete and permanent marital failure. They are both an outcome of the same approach, contrary to a too easily obtainable divorce, and aimed at preservation of marriage unions whenever possible. The intention to save the marriages which appear before the divorce court has come out in the above mentioned procedural provisions. According to them the court, at the very beginning of each divorce suit, has to summon the parties to a conciliatory session, where the judge shall induce them to become reconciled. The court may forego the session only in the event of serious difficulties which hinder either spouse from appearing before the court. The duty to attempt reconciliation is not limited to this session; further efforts should be made by the court during the whole course of the trial, to reconcile the spouses, whenever possible. All these provisions indicate that the divorce court is not a body invested only for making arbitrary decisions. It has also been entrusted with another function of import: the application of therapy in cases of maladjusted marriages.

As a matter of fact, a divorce trial is not the best moment to use therapy: it should be applied by the marriage counselling centres at an earlier stage of marital conflict. However, these centres are only just starting their activities in Poland. The lack of properly developed marriage counselling is a real dilemma: the data gathered in the course of these investigations prove how urgently those whose marriages have become unhappy need competent and friendly advice and mediation; they also throw some light on the harmful effects which appear if this need is not met. For want of properly arranged marriage counselling, the divorce court is only agency whose duty it is to attempt reconciliation.

1.2. The real value of the court's conciliatory proceedings has become a matter of skeptical conjectures under those legal systems which have introduced it. This has been the case in France, Germany, Switzerland, Austria and various other countries. This has also been the case in Poland, and skepticism has concerned, in particular, the main element of the proceedings: the conciliatory session. Several legal writers have pointed out that "the conciliatory session, in its present form, has not stood up to the test" [1], and has given hardly perceptible results [2]: "it is usually limited... to a brief examination of the parties... followed by the stereotyped question whether they do not see any chance of reconciliation; a laconic negative answer fully satisfies the court..., thus the session becomes... an unnecessary formality" [3]. These views, published in the years 1959/1960, refer to the previous opinions expressed under the rule of the Law of Marriage of 1945 [4]. Already then the sessions had been called 'a waste of energy'; for, to be able to initiate effective conciliatory activity, the judge "would have to know both spouses well..., would have to become acquainted with their characters..., the character and course of the conflict as well as its causes, often deeply hidden, would have to gain the immediate and full confidence of the couple with whom he is making contact for the first time. He would have to induce the spouses to make sincere disclosures. He should also have great power of persuasion... In fact, a conjunction of all those elements, the more so in a session where the judge has 20–30 cases of this kind, is completely improbable" [5].

The above opinions seem justified, in particular in the light of methods used and experience collected by marriage counselling centres in those countries where marriage counselling has become a highly developed social service. However, they certainly are in disaccord with

[1] T. Misiuk, "W kregu spraw rozwodowych" ("On Divorce Problems") in *Prawo i Zycie* (1960/15), p. 2.

[2] Z. Resich, "Dyskutujemy nad projektem kodeksu postepowania cywilnego" ("Discussing the Draft Code of Civil Procedure") in *Prawo i Zycie* (1960/11), p. 3.

[3] J. Rajski, "Gwarancje procesowe prawidłowego rozpatrywania i rozstrzygania spraw rozwodowych" ("The Procedural Safeguards of Proper Considering and Deciding the Divorce Cases") in *Nowe Prawo* (1959/7-8), pp. 871, 872.

[4] Which preceded the Family Code of 1950.

[5] Z. Garlicki, "Posiedzenia pojednawcze" ("Conciliatory Sessions") in *Demokratyczny Przeglad Prawniczy* (1948/8), p. 17.

the factual data made available to me by the Statistical Department of the Ministry of Justice. According to those data, reconciliation in a divorce suit occurs quite frequently. Table 6 shows the figures.

TABLE 6

Proportion of Discontinuations of Proceedings Caused by Reconciliation to Finally Concluded Divorce Trials in Poland

Year	TOTALS	Divorce decree	Dismissal	Discontinuation of proceedings caused by reconciliation	Discontinuation of proceedings caused by other reasons
1959	19 344	15 422	2009	748	1165
1960	18 706	14 882	1903	730	1191
1961	20 015	16 407	1759	690	1159
1962	21 389	17 954	1770	788	887
1963	23 273	19 455	1856	897	1065

The above table indicates that, in 1959, the proportion of discontinuations of proceedings caused by reconciliation amounted to 4.0 per cent of all the finally concluded divorce suits, in 1960 it was 3.9, in 1961 – 3.4, in 1962 – 3.7, in 1963 – 3.8 per cent. Ranging between 3.4 and 4.0 per cent, the proportion is high enough to bring into doubt those opinions which deny the effectiveness of the court's conciliatory proceedings. What is, then, the real value of the proceedings? To learn this is the purpose of the present enquiry.

2. THE CONCILIATORY SESSION

2.1. *The Impact of the Degree of Breakdown on the Chance of Reconciliation*

The conciliatory session is not a separate entity, but an element of a more complex structure: of the whole of conflict between the spouses. That is why its effectiveness is dependent not only upon the way it is conducted, but also upon the intensity of conflict. The more intense the conflict, the slighter the chance of reconciliation, and if a marriage has become a complete failure, even the most skilful conciliatory efforts cannot result in recovery.

I did not estimate, for the use of the present considerations, the degree of breakdown between the divorcing couples in the period immediately preceding the conciliatory session. It is therefore not known in what proportion of trials attended the degree of breakdown was so insignificant that there was a real chance of reconciliation. Yet, it may be supposed that the degree is usually considerable. This is indicated by the fact of filing the petition: the decision of starting the divorce suit is mostly an effect of serious conflict. Moreover, the filing of a petition, indicating an intense conflict, frequently becomes an additional factor contributing to its growth. There are two reasons for this. Firstly, it is an act of determined decision on the part of the plaintiff, withdrawal from which may be difficult. Secondly, it sometimes provokes the defendant, and, in effect, aggravates the relations between the spouses. All the 131 divorcees interviewed were asked: "Did the divorce suit as such make relations between you and your partner more bitter than they had been before it began?". Those in whose opinion it did, were asked to say why. A detailed report on the answers obtained will be given below. At present it is sufficient to mention that 14 divorcees, i.e. 10.7 per cent of the sample interviewed, said that the very fact of filing the petition intensified the conflict. 8 of them gave as the reason mainly the contents of the petition: "the wife's words were so offensive that it was difficult not to bear her a grudge" (D-52); "the petition indicated that my wife had done everything with premeditation and had not loved me..., it has been so painful" (D-100); "it finally repelled me that my wife was able to lie that way, not only had she been unfaithful, but she had made me seem a scoundrel...; I thought she was silly, fickle, simply young, and it appeared that she had a vile character" (D-111). The further 6 subjects found the very fact of filing the petition was an embittering circumstance: "my husband had a grudge against me for filing the petition" (D-17), "he had a grudge, started to beat me, and was constantly at me for having done it" (D-35), the husband "made me upset by the fact that the affair had reached the court; it was not the proper place to settle our marriage problems" (D-110).

The bringing of a divorce suit is, then, usually the result of a serious conflict, and sometimes it makes the conflict even more intense. However, it is clear, particularly in the light of the factual data presented in the previous part of this study, that the bringing of not every divorce suit implies completeness and permanency, or even a high degree of breakdown. Though I did not estimate the degree of breakdown in the period preceding the conciliatory session, the present investigations indicate that in some proportion of trials, a minority, but still quite considerable, the degree is so low that there does exist a real chance of reconciliation. It is evident that this chance appears first in those cases where the spouses eventually become reconciled: according to the above mentioned data drawn from the Ministry of Justice, they amount to 3.4 – 4.0 per cent of all the finally concluded divorce suits. This chance appears, moreover, in the trials which result in dismissal because of the absence of breakdown. In my sample of 153 trials attended 11 final dismissals were decreed, and in 3 of them the want of an irreparable breakdown of marriage constituted the ground for dismissal. The chance of reconciliation also appears sometimes in those relatively few cases which, contrary to the provisions in force, result in pronouncement of divorce in spite of the fact that the breakdown has not become complete and permanent. Lastly, it appears in the cases where the breakdown is not considerable in the period preceding the conciliatory session, but then, as result of embitterment caused by the further course of the trial, it grows to such a degree that the court eventually has to pronounce divorce; the aggravating influence of the further course of the trial, as well as its impact on the intensity of breakdown, will be considered below. In all the situations mentioned here the therapeutic activity of the divorce court falls on fertile ground; and making use of the chance of reconciliation depends upon the manner in which this activity is carried out.

2.2. *The Structure of the Conciliatory Session*

2.2.1. Several persons take part in the conciliatory session. There is always a judge among them, in principle the same one who will conduct the case in its further course. He sits behind the judicial table, on an elevated platform, in a robe with a chain of office on his breast, separated by a balustrade from the spouses who speak with him standing. This makes for a feeling of distance, quite the opposite of the informal, easy atmosphere which the marriage counselling centres have always been so careful to ensure. Both spouses take part in the session together: this results in constraint on both sides and inclines them to hide from the judge those circumstances which either spouse intends to hide from his partner. The presence of two laymen and of a recorder increases the constraint. One of the judges who conducted the suits attended, did not fully observe the principle of closed doors: he admitted some other persons to the session, in particular undergraduates of law who were serving an apprenticeship in the court. It is clear that in this way, and especially in the presence of so many persons, the proper atmosphere is not created.

Some of the judges interviewed were aware of this: they were for limiting of the number of participants, and believed that "less official methods should be used..., the judge should act as a mediator, not as an authority" (J-17). It is interesting that sometimes even the divorcees feel the need of a more informal atmosphere, and especially the limiting of the number of persons taking part in the session; "it would possibly be better if such talks were arranged not in the courtroom, because there one feels too unsettled, but more confidentially", said one of the divorced women; "if they had spoken with my husband possibly he would have changed, he was not a bad man, but had not been well brought up, because he had run away from his parents' home and grew up alone" (D-74). "I felt like a poor orphan before the court", confessed another woman interviewed, "beauty and refinement mean so much to me. That nasty interior, that high judicial table, the faces of so many men..., I never felt so lonely before... Why does the court separate itself from us by a balustrade, why does it overwhelm us, simple, poor people? Should it necessarily strike awe into us instead of encouraging us to apply to it for assistance and protection?" (D-124).

2.2.2. The conciliatory sessions are called two different ways. Some of the judges call one or a few sessions at a time in the intervals between the trials; others set aside a whole day for a larger number of sessions. The latter plan from 25 to 35 sessions per day. This method determines the time limits of the sessions: the 84 sessions attended lasted from 4 to 25 minutes, with the mean value of 12.2, the median of 11.5 minutes. According to the information furnished by the judges and barristers from Warsaw, Lublin and Katowice, in none of those courts do the conciliatory sessions last longer.

On the ground of Art. 436 Para. 2 of the Code of Civil Procedure, "if the conciliatory session does not result in reconciliation, and if adjournment of the session would be of no avail, the judge... shall declare that the conciliatory activities have produced no effect". This norm provides adjournments of conciliatory sessions, i.e. the use of a therapy similar, at least in its time structure, to the activities of the marriage counselling centres. However, this intention is not realized in court practice: there was no adjournment in any of the 84 sessions attended. In order to learn whether adjournments sometimes take place I asked every judge interviewed whether repeated conciliatory sessions had occurred in his practice. 35 of the 41 judges gave negative answer, the remaining 6 remembered altogether 15 adjournments. Those 15 adjournments amounted to 0.05 per cent of all the conciliatory sessions conducted by all the judges interviewed.

An evident regularity appears in the structure of the conciliatory session: it is generally composed of 3 parts. The first consists in an attempt to diagnose the conflict. The second – in the judge's conciliatory activities. The third – in his activities directed to the organization of the further course of the trial. These parts, usually following the same sequence, are easily distinguishable; however, sometimes their elements alternate so that the borders between them become blurred.

2.3. *The Diagnosis*

2.3.1. It would be difficult to reconcile the spouses without learning the character of conflict between them. That is why an attempt at diagnosing the conflict is an initial part of the majority of conciliatory sessions. Various judges attempt it in different manners. In the Cracow Court two methods came to light. The first of them consists in treating the petition, and sometimes the defendant's answer, provided that it has been put forward in writing, as the main or the only source of information; the second, in the collecting of more detailed data. The first method has been adopted by 3 of the judges, the second by the other 3.

The judges who diagnose on the basis of the petition proceed according to a simplified scheme. One of them limits himself to reading the petition at the beginning of each session, and not only refrains from demanding any further explanations, but, moreover, does not allow the parties to tell anything about the character of the conflict, even if they wanted to. It is not till the later part of the session that the parties, asked about the possibility of reconciliation, now and then spontaneously reveal some data: "I won't become reconciled because the wife has an illegitimate child" (CS-58), "because she committed a criminal offence" (CS-82), because "I am suffering schizophrenia" (CS-71). However, the judge does not even want to hear this information to the end if it is likely to be a little more extensive. Thus, when the plaintiff, asked whether he "would like to become reconciled with his wife" answers: "I should have to speak about that for a long time", the judge says: "briefly and concisely, do you want to become reconciled?" (CS-74); and when a defendant wife, asked about "any possibility of reconciliation", started to present her own version of the conflict, inconsistent with the petition, the judge interrupted her: "yes, but now the court is bound to ask you only whether you want to become reconciled with your husband" (CS-80). The attitude of the second of those judges who diagnose on the basis of the petition is even more radical: he reads the petition before the conciliatory session, and at the session he immediately begins to reconcile the parties. The third judge treats the diagnostic part of the session rather broadly. He first asks the plaintiff if he does not want to become reconciled, and then, on receiving a negative answer, whether the reasons for refusal are those which have been given in the petition. If the plaintiff says that this is the case, the judge presents the petition to the laymen and then asks the defendant whether he would like to become reconciled, and whether the statements contained in the petition are true. If the defendant insists they are not, the judge asks him to present his own version of the case; then he turns, if necessary, to the plaintiff again, asking him for further explanations. This way the judge frequently obtains information which goes beyond the contents of the petition; nevertheless, even here, the reading of the petition constitutes the main element of the diagnostic activities.

The remaining 3 judges do not limit themselves to the reading of the petition and, sometimes, the defendant's answer. One of them, upon learning that the plaintiff does not want to become reconciled "because of the reasons given in the petition", is never satisfied with such a declaration, demands an oral presentation of the reasons, and then asks the defendant to give his opinion of the plaintiff's words. The last two give more time than the others to diagnosing the conflict. They always ask some diagnostic questions, the contents of which depends on contents of the petition and on the information furnished by the parties in the course of the session. The questions range from quite general ones: "how did you live together?" (CS-17), "why don't you want to live with your wife?" (CS-27), "what fault do you impute to your wife?" (CS-14), to much more detailed questions, concerning unfaithfulness, insults, drinking, beating, motives for getting married, economic conditions of the parties if it seems that they have contributed to the breakdown of the marriage; in a case in which, according to the plaintiff's words, "the wife has been suffering from a nervous disease", the judge asks her several questions in order to examine her mental state (CS-13). If the spouses, having refused to become reconciled, spontaneously give reasons for the refusal or answer the above questions, the judges do not interrupt them for quite a while: thus the parties who do want to present the elements of conflict are allowed to do so, and if they are inclined to unburden themselves, they make known a great deal of data.

2.3.2. The above survey of judicial diagnostic activities displays some of its deficiencies. The first of them is lack of time: the experience of marriage counselling centres indicates how much time is needed to diagnose the conflict properly. The second is the incompetence of the judges: to diagnose the conflict, it is not so much a legal education that is necessary, as those traits and abilities which characterize marriage counsellors, in particular a knowledge of the peculiar structure of discords in the family, and the ability to establish intimate contact with the spouses; yet judges are neither selected nor trained from this point of view. More will be said below as to how strongly the parties feel the lack of time and the incompetence of the judges at the conciliatory session. It is also felt by the barristers of all the courts examined: "the judges arrange 30-35 sessions per day; for want of time they do not ask about anything, they are familiar only with the petition, and not with the very roots of conflict" (B-25); "at the conciliatory session the court should learn the causes of breakdown; for that purpose the parties should be interrogated in a more detailed manner..., much more time is necessary, now there are 30-40 sessions per day" (B-59); "it is conducted by young people without experience, who moreover do not know anything about the case in which they induce to reconciliation" (B-36).

The judges' want of knowledge is caused not only by lack of time and abilities. At the conciliatory session they diagnose the conflict mainly on the ground of the declarations of the parties, and the more sincere those declarations are, the easier it is to make the proper diagnosis. However, the conciliatory session is an element of the divorce suit, and is conducted by the same judge who will, in future, pronounce the decree, i.e. make the decision as to the procedural goals of the parties. Hence – a peculiar antinomy: the parties should be sincere to enable the judge to diagnose the conflict, but reasons of procedural tactics often incline them to hide the truth. I have said above how the parties, in order to achieve their procedural goals, deceive the court and hide the truth from it in the further course of the divorce suit. It is obvious that, due to including the conciliatory session in the trial itself, the deceiving and hiding appear at the session also. It came out in particular in the interviews of divorcees. 9 of them, when describing the course of the session, said – spontaneously, since they were not asked about it – that they had hidden the truth from the court because of tactical reasons: the judge, having aimed at reconciliation, "could not use the proper arguments, because... he did not know the real circumstances of our break-up, which we had hidden" (D-12); "the husband gave as a reason for divorce the fact that I did not want to take care of his child; possibly that was why the judge did not insist on reconciliation..., that reason was sham, but we had agreed on it in common with the barrister" (D-76); "the judge tried to bring us to reconciliation using set phrases, without understanding, without any knowledge of the subject matter and of the intellectual level of those to whom he addressed himself..., it was difficult to treat him seriously..., he got on with his business, and we three, the wife, the barrister and I, carried through what we wanted" (D-14).

2.4. *Conciliatory Activity*

2.4.1. The conciliatory activities are the most important part of the session. The effort at conciliation varies: it ranges from lack of any serious effort to a great one. A difference in attitude is the reason for this. Some of the judges maintain a skeptical attitude: they do not believe it possible to have any real influence on the behaviour of the parties. This opinion is a result of their experience: they become aware of lack of success in their conciliatory activities, and they explain this state of affairs by the intensity of the marital conflict between those who start a divorce suit, by the briefness of the conciliatory session, the impossibility of making a proper diagnosis, and their own want of skill. I asked all the 41 judges interviewed whether, in their opinion, the conciliatory session should be maintained in its present form, rejected, or modified. Moreover, I asked for reasons for the opinions expressed, and those who were for modification were requested to say what changes they would make. Lastly, I asked all the judges what they used to say to the parties at the session. 16 of them believed that the conciliatory activities were completely hopeless, and therefore they were firmly for doing away with the sessions; in their opinion the sessions were a "useless fiction" (J-27), "unimportant formality" (J-21), "unnecessary waste of time" (J-41), the more so that those who enter into a divorce suit "are usually firmly decided to divorce" (J-40), and consider the protraction of the trial caused by the conciliatory session a "chicanery which does not calm them, but makes them more irritated" (J-5).

The opposite of this attitude is the hopeful approach: the belief that the conciliatory session gives a real chance of reconciliation. It seems that this belief is usually a result of the personal traits of some, not numerous judges, who are able to establish contact with the parties easily, who have intuition, the capacity for arguing, experience, and moreover are, to a greater degree than the others, inclined to help the spouses. They succeed in their conciliatory activities more frequently than those skeptically disposed, and in this way find, in the outcome of their own extra efforts, support for their attitude. This attitude was made known by 11 of the judges interviewed. They were definitely for maintaining the conciliatory session in its present form, because, in their opinion, the session "fulfills its conciliatory function well" (J-3). They also mentioned their own efforts at conciliation: "I ask the plaintiff whether he would not think over his decision, I ask the defendant whether he would like to become reconciled, if the plaintiff does not want to, I ask him to make known his charges against the defendant, then I use arguments which depend upon the circumstances in a given case..., I very conscientiously induce to reconciliation whenever there are children, I sometimes bring the parents to tears" (J-8); "if I see that there is some hope, I don't spare time..., I sometimes explain various things to people, they talk about their sufferings and give vent to their emotions" (J-15): "I speak with the parties not like a judge, but informally..., if they feel the need of speaking – and people want to pour themselves out – I enable them to talk about their troubles, and I try, in a longer conversation, to reconcile and to explain" (J-10).

Obviously between those two extremes there are intermediate attitudes, and it seems probable that they had been adopted by some of the remaining 14 judges interviewed. Their answers were, however, too vague to enable me, without collecting more detailed information on their behaviour at the sessions, to determine their attitudes clearly: they limited themselves, for the most part, to saying that the session should be maintained, because "it sometimes helps" (J-4), or "possibly might help in a given case" (J-9), and some of them were for modifying it, in particular for conducting it only at the request of either party, in the period preceding the divorce suit, before the filing of petition embitters the relations between the spouses. However, each of those 14 subjects could have been included, on the ground of a more detailed analysis of his conduct, in the skeptical or hopeful group, depending on which of the two groups his behaviour approached more nearly. Hence the attitudes of all the judges will be reduced to the above two models.

2.4.2. There are in the Cracow Court 4 judges who represent the skeptical attitude. They made this known in the interviews: 2 of them were for rejecting the conciliatory session, 2 others declared for maintaining it, but with evident hesitation. It was, however, mainly their behaviour in the course of the sessions attended which disclosed their attitude: they usually perform the conciliatory activities without making any effort. One of them limited himself to asking about the possibility of reconciliation, and never insisted when the answer was a refusal. Another, for the most part, behaved in a like manner; nevertheless, in 6 of the 15 observed sessions conducted by him, he made a slight effort to bring the parties to reconciliation. In particular, to a plaintiff complaining that the wife did not satisfy him, the judge said: "she did satisfy you for so many years..., you have a common son, perhaps, after all, you could become reconciled" (CS-56). In another case he said to the plaintiff wife: "perhaps you could come to a reconciliation, we shall suspend the proceedings for 3 months..., perhaps you will both change" (CS-57). The third judge also only went beyond simple questions as to the possibility of reconciliation in a few cases, and, in 4 out of 15 observed sessions conducted by him, the slightness of his conciliatory activities was, considering the parties' lack of resolve to divorce, difficult to justify. Thus, when in the above mentioned case CS-74 the plaintiff husband, asked about the possibility of reconciliation, answered he "would have to speak about it for a long time", and the defendant wife wanted to become reconciled, the judge neither let the plaintiff speak nor made any attempt to bring the parties to reconciliation. Similarly, there was no such attempt in two further sessions in spite of the fact that the plaintiff husbands, when asked about the possibility of reconciliation, seemed to hesitate, and the defendants were for reconciliation. Lastly, in the case CS-70, the plaintiff wife said: "I possibly would agree to reconciliation, but is there any chance? And will any good come of it?", and the defendant answered: "I would like to be reconciled, I married in order to have a good and normal family, but it doesn't work, my wife constantly storms at me". Having heard these words the judge limited himself to asking the same question three times: "will you, then, come to reconciliation or not?"; he moreover said: "you have three children", and subsequently he turned to the wife: "one should not use vulgar words, it is not nice and is harmful to the children".

The last of the 4 judges whom I am considering, unlike the others, always attempts to bring the spouses to reconciliation, but, according to him, he does it from sense of duty, without hope of succeeding, and the arguments he used were not convincing. He said, in case CS-65: "it is true that you don't have children, but, after all, it is a marriage, have you thought it over? Wouldn't you return to the common life?". At two further sessions he limited the conciliatory activities to one sentence solemnly pronounced: "the court appeals to the parties to become reconciled, marriage should be a lasting union, the more so if there is a little child" (CS-58, 68). Lastly, in the case CS-59, both parties behaved in the manner indicating the want of any definite decision to divorce. Since the plaintiff husband had adopted, at the time of marriage, the wife's child, the judge said: "you have a common child, another child has been adopted by the husband, is there not any possibility of reconciliation? Divorce is, after all, an extreme step". Seeing the parties hesitate, the judge continued: "Well, you don't hate each other, do you?"; and then having learned that the plaintiff, overloaded with welfare work had neglected the family, and that there had been quarrels between the parties, he added: "yes, in marriage quarrels occur..., but perhaps you will think it over before you come to the court again". The plaintiff said to that: "do not call us too early, please", the judge proposed suspension of proceedings, and the parties accepted the proposal. Then the judge turned to them once again: "do think it over, please, perhaps the marriage could be saved for the good of the children". Having concluded this way he did not help them to learn and evaluate the real elements of the conflict nor in working out any plans for strengthening their union; he did not even properly exploit those conciliatory arguments offered by the parties themselves: neither did he use as an argument the relation of the plaintiff to the defendant's illegitimate child nor the fact that care for wife and children is a duty no less important than those for which the plaintiff had neglected the family. The parties, having found no assistance and advice, left the courtroom without the prospect of divorce and without any new prospect of reconciliation, with a feeling of complete helplessness written on their faces.

2.4.3. The remaining two judges represent a hopeful approach: these are the two who diagnose the conflict more carefully than the others. The intensity of their conciliatory activities depends on the effects of the diagnostic part of the session: if these results lead them to believe that there is a chance of reconciliation, they spare no effort. In such a case the first of them uses various arguments suited to the situation of the parties. In the case where an almost 60-year-old plaintiff had deserted an ill wife and sickly child, the judge called attention to his age with a severe benevolence, and persuaded him to take care of his wife: "you want a divorce? An old man and he wants a divorce? How old are you?... You have an ill wife and a child..., since your wife suffers from a nervous disease, you should take care of her, and not seek divorce" (CS-13). To a plaintiff who had himself infringed the marital duties, the judge said: "You won't become reconciled with your wife? You are guilty, and you, besides that, want a divorce? You should come to reconciliation..., you are standing so near your wife, ask her to forgive you" (CS-9). This judge earnestly persuaded a defendant wife, a habitual card player, to promise before the court she would give up gambling for the good of the children, and he tried to explain to a plaintiff, who obsessively suspected his wife of unfaithfulness, that the suspicions were possibly groundless, and that "one should trust one's wife" (CS-24). He was particularly scrupulous in his efforts to bring an old mountaineer couple to reconciliation, adapting the language used and the atmosphere of the session to the parties' way of thinking: "Why did you come to the court", he asked the defendant husband, "do you beat your woman?... Do you love your woman?"; and when the defendant, who was against divorce, said he had never beaten, and had always loved her, the judge turned to her: "you see, your husband loves you, you should return to the common life". She replied aggressively, said he had beaten her, then she started a dispute with him over money, a cow, real property, but the judge interrupted her: "42 years have elapsed since your wedding, you will wait till 50 have passed and have your golden wedding..., all this brings shame on you in the eyes of the village..., well, go on, kiss the woman". The defendant tried to embrace her, she pushed him away, and the judge continued: "don't be so hard, one should forgive, human beings make mistakes, commit sins; he will beg you forgiveness, we shall suspend the proceedings for three months and make one more attempt, there will be a period for improvement, he shall be good to you". When she subsequently refused to become reconciled and claimed immediate division of the matrimonial property [6], the judge added that "not property, but the human being is important in marriage" (CS-23).

The second of these judges who represent the hopeful approach

[6] In Poland the community of acquests is the statutory régime (see on this my article, "Matrimonial Property in Poland", *Modern Law Review* (1963/2), p. 156 et seq.).

conducts the conciliatory session with particular skill. He is an intelligent man, inspires confidence, creates an informal, kind atmosphere. He has considerable experience from which he draws a number of conciliatory arguments, general enough to be adapted to a variety of cases, and, on the other hand, particular enough not to be complete commonplaces. The number of such arguments is, obviously, limited, and they are repeated; but the parties do not know this and may believe that the judge's words have been spoken this way for them only. The arguments are of different kinds. There is sometimes an appeal to the parental feelings of the parties, in particular calling attention to the injury and wrong done to the children as a result of divorce, to difficulties connected with their age, to their "right to have parents; you contracted marriage to bring up the children, they should grow up better than you are" (CS-34); besides they will "have a deep grudge" against the plaintiff who, because of another woman, tried to get a divorce (CS-33). In two cases the judge used a metaphor: the hour the clock of the parties' life has struck. I had also heard this metaphor in the pilot study, and, moreover, it appeared in the further course of the trials attended, when the judge returned to an attempt at reconciliation. The hour changed: if the parties were old it was evening, if they were young – noon, but the time was always late enough to induce to reflection. This figurative argument, brought forward in a suggestive voice, sometimes apparently influenced the parties. Several times the judge used other arguments drawn from the peculiar situation of the parties. He said, in the case of a country family, where the husband, having kept everything under lock and key, did not admit the wife to any functions in the household: "go to the wife and give her the keys to everything. Do not interfere in what will be cooked for dinner, it is a woman's business, do what should be done by a husband"; then he turned to the wife: "and you should care for your husband, friendliness is necessary" (CS-27). He emphatically pointed out the value of affection. He said to the plaintiff whose wife declared she loved him and therefore she was against divorce: "you are going to lose a great blessing, you have a woman who loves you, you will meet many women, but not such a one who will love you" (CS-33); "your wife says she loves you, no other woman will love you in need" (CS-36). In the last case the judge made an attempt to rouse the parties to greater activity in tending towards reconciliation: "you must find the proper way yourselves, you are guardians of this union". He had a lengthy conversation with the parties who said, on entering for the session, that they wanted to become reconciled. Enabling them to speak broadly and to unburden themselves, he treated the court as a friendly institution: "it is a very good thing that you come with your problem to the court". He asked the plaintiff wife not to forget "that the husband was in Auschwitz and his nerves have been affected"; and he asked the defendant to keep in mind that the wife had waited for his return "and her nerves are also affected...; please, do fight against the wish to have even one drink, I have a great tragedy in my family too, I fight my troubles and the struggle brings results"; in emphasizing his own experience, the judge probably aimed at increasing confidence in his competence and the value of his advice, and, moreover, he was trying to approach the parties on the ground of similarity of experiences. He also skilfully pointed out the necessity of guarding the affections: "this is an appeal to the heart (not that you have no affection, I know you love each other, but) one should tend the affections (which relates rather to younger couples than to you), more serenity, more smiles, it sounds like a commonplace, but in fact it is not". Having used such arguments he moved the parties so much that they left the courtroom kissing each other, and the defendant asked, crying, to be allowed to remain in touch with the judge in order to obtain his advice in the future (CS-26).

2.4.4. Both the above presented attitudes of the judges came out in information furnished by the divorcees. And, oddly enough, both were also disclosed in information furnished by reconciled persons, although one would have expected that all the reconciled couples had met only the hopeful, not the skeptical approach in the conciliatory session; this was, however, not the case, and mention will be made below of how the parties were brought to reconciliation despite the want of any effort on the part of the judge. All the divorced and reconciled persons were asked: "do you remember the conciliatory session, i.e. the first sitting in the court, at which the judge tried to bring you to reconciliation?" Those who did remember were subsequently asked: "how did the judge try to bring you to reconciliation?". 137 subjects in all were asked the above questions: 124 divorced and 13 reconciled. The remaining 7 divorcees had not taken part in a conciliatory session; the court had omitted the session because of various difficulties: the prolonged illness of either party, absence abroad or detention in prison, persistent refusal to appear in the court.

The answers of 52 subjects did not throw much light on the behaviour of the judges who had conducted their divorce suits. Some of those subjects did not remember the conciliatory arguments used by the judge, the others limited themselves to quoting the arguments used so briefly that any evaluation of the judicial effort at conciliation was impossible; some of them said that, in fact, the judge's conciliatory activity had not been great, but that the want of effort may well have been due to the apparent hopelessness of the case.

A further 54 subjects interviewed furnished information indicating the slightness or complete want of effort on the part of the judge: "the judge asked whether we wanted to become reconciled, heard that we didn't and went no further" (D-4); "the judge asked only whether we agreed to divorce, he did not say anything more, there was no attempt to reconcile..., everything proceeded in the greatest hurry" (D-45); "it was conducted very quickly, because there were to be 32 further sessions after us, that was probably why the judge had no time for a longer conversation" (D-78); "the session lasted just a moment, it was got out of the way, I did not know anything about reconciliation, you [7] are the first to tell me that they should have induced us to become reconciled" (D-75); "it was simply a formality" (D-44); the judge spoke "without conviction, it sounded like a set formula" (D-59). The words 'formality', 'formula', appeared 16 times in the interviews of the 54 subjects, and 4 of them were not aware of the conciliatory character of the session, and maintained, contrary to the contents of the court records, that in their cases there was no conciliatory session at all. Lastly, one of the women interviewed revealed a particularly painful instance of the effect of the judge's skeptical attitude. She filed petition not in order to obtain a divorce, but to become reconciled. She hoped her husband would be shocked and frightened by her step and that then the court would bring the parties to reconciliation; but the judge "did not make any attempt at conciliation at all" (D-103). This case, as well as another one mentioned above [8], is an outcome of a broader tendency which, in the course of my inquiry, came to light in the courtroom as well: the spouses are sometimes inclined to use the divorce suit as remedy for their marriage. This tendency seems to be an outcome of the unfulfilled need for advice and mediation, and the hope of finding the adviser and mediator in the person of the judge.

It is obvious that these critical opinions should be treated with caution. Sometimes it is the petition itself and the behaviour of the parties at the session which indicate that the marriage cannot be saved, and justify

[7] i.e. the interviewer.

[8] On p. 71.

the lack of conciliatory effort. However, even then those of the subjects interviewed who, despite the hopelessness of the case, deeply desired to save their union, could not understand and therefore disapproved of the judge's lack of conciliatory activities. Moreover, the party strongly opposing the pronouncement of divorce may sometimes expect an extraordinary effort on the part of the judge, and therefore find even a considerable effort insignificant. Nevertheless, it seems that the majority of the above opinions reflect a real shortcoming in conciliatory activity; the more so because 27 opinions were those of plaintiffs, who obviously were not defending themselves against divorce.

The remaining 31 subjects spoke of considerable efforts at conciliation on the part of the judge. Some of them quoted the conciliatory arguments used by him, the others limited themselves to a general description of his behaviour: "the judge did everything to reconcile us" (D-85); "it was evident that he did his best and that it was not a mere formality" (D-129); he showed "great conscientiousness in inducing us to become reconciled..., someone less stubborn than I am would have given up and been moved" (D-13); "they persuaded us very earnestly..., they said that we had been married for so long, that perhaps we would still seek a reconciliation, that we should not make up our minds recklessly; I was surprised that the judge put himself to so much trouble, I had imagined that it would be a formality, and he spoke about it more or less half an hour" (D-5); "he spoke quite earnestly; if we had been undecided we probably would have given up and become reconciled" (D-80); "he spoke so that I was ready to agree to reconciliation..., there is time enough between the conciliatory session and the subsequent sitting of the court; if there had been any improvement on the part of the husband, I would have withdrawn the petition" (D-20); "the judge who conducted our case was simply charming, he spoke to us like a father, he said to my husband: 'please, look at your wife, where will you find another so pretty, so nice, kiss her and do not think about divorce any more, you seem made for each other'. We both were nearly weeping" (R-8).

There were in all 85 subjects who spoke in this way about the attitudes of the judges who had conducted the conciliatory sessions: the skeptical approach was mentioned by 54 persons, the hopeful – by 31. It would be interesting to determine the correlation between the attitude of various judges which I had noticed in the courtroom, and their attitude in the eyes of the subjects interviewed. This correlation cannot be measured with regard to all the judges. For, the conciliatory sessions at which the subjects interviewed were induced to reconciliation took place in the first months of 1959, the conciliatory sessions attended – three years later, and in the meantime some part of the divorce judges had changed: in 1962 there remained only 3 of those who had been in charge in 1959; the estimation of the correlation between their attitudes observed by myself, and the attitudes described by the subjects interviewed was only practicable in the case of those three.

Those 3 judges conducted the majority of the divorce suits in 1959: therefore 77 of the 85 subjects interviewed had taken part in the conciliatory sessions conducted by them. One of them has been classified above, on my observation, in the skeptical group, two in the hopeful group. 24 subjects had met the skeptical judge at the conciliatory session: 22 of them told of the lack or scantiness of his efforts at conciliation, and only 2 told of a considerable effort. 53 subjects had met the two remaining judges: 25 of them mentioned want or scantiness of effort, and as many as 28 – considerable effort. Table 7 shows these figures.

TABLE 7

The Attitude of Judges in the Light of my Observation and their Attitude in the Eyes of Divorced and Reconciled Persons

The attitude of the judge / Information of subjects interviewed	The skeptical judge	The two hopeful judges
The subjects telling of want of considerable effort at conciliation	22	25
The subjects telling of considerable effort at conciliation	2	28
TOTALS	24	53

These figures confirm the data collected in the courtroom; they clearly show the difference in attitudes of the judges. It is a significant difference: $X^2 = 13.76$ ($P < 0.05$, $df = 1$).

2.5. *Organization of Trial*

The conciliatory session is the first contact of the court with the parties: it therefore affords an opportunity of taking measures to render the further course of the suit more efficient. This opportunity is taken by all the judges observed. They undertake two kinds of organizing activity. First they try to get some general information as to the structure of the suit, in particular whether it will be contested or uncontested, and, in the case of contest, what will be the object of dispute; having got this information, they can make some conjecture as to how much time a given trial will take, how much evidence will be needed, and, consequently, how to arrange the dates and duration of sittings. The inclination of some judges to put an end to contest is connected with this: I have mentioned above how they induce the parties to agree as to the procedural goals. This inducement, if it takes place, constitutes an important element in the organizing of the session.

Various court orders form a further element. There are, in particular, orders to complete the information contained in the petition, to put forward an answer, to present documents, to give addresses of witnesses, etc. There are sometimes also temporary decisions which organize not so much the further course of the suit as relations in the broken family during its course, in particular decisions concerning the amount of alimony due to either spouse from his partner or due to the children.

All these elements appear not only in the Cracow Court, but also in the other courts under investigation. According to the information furnished by the judges and barristers interviewed, the conciliatory session is, in all the courts, "useful as a preliminary survey of the case" (J-34), the more so that "during the session a decision is reached as to whether there will be an agreement on the procedural goals or a contest" (B-33), "the session affords an opportunity to make decisions" concerning the duty to pay alimony (J-32), it "organizes the trial" (J-3), "it forms the further course of the suit" (B-27). Hence, some of the judges and barristers who in the interviews denied the effectiveness of the session as a conciliatory measure, were for its continuation as a means of making the further course of the trial more efficient.

3. THE CONCILIATORY ACTIVITY OF THE COURT IN THE FURTHER COURSE OF THE DIVORCE TRIAL

3.1. *The Chance of Reconciliation*

3.1.1. In the further course of the divorce suit there appear some circumstances which influence the probability of reconciliation. Two of them have a favourable influence. The first is the lapse of time: It is the cooling-off period following the conciliatory session which is particularly favourable to reflection and emotional appeasement. Moreover, during the further course of the trial various changes in all the circumstances of the parties' lives can occur; more will be said below about their possible influence on the decision to divorce. Another factor which may increase the chance of reconciliation is the judge's gathering of evidence which sometimes enables him to diagnose the conflict properly, and, consequently, to choose the proper moment for, and the proper way of bringing the parties into harmony.

3.1.2. However, in the further course of the trial, there also appears another factor, which decreases the probability of reconciliation: this is the embittering influence of the trial. Several factors contribute to this. The first of them is the behaviour of the parties. I have said above to what degree the very fact of filing a petition intensifies the conflict. The above described charges which appear in the further course of the trial, in particular in the courtroom, make it still more intense, as do the charges of barristers and witnesses, which seem to be no less embittering than those brought by the spouses themselves; for the barristers and witnesses are, for the most part, instigated by the party, and that is why the other party has a self-evident inclination to impute all they have said to the initiative of his partner. The faults of which parties were accused in the course of the trials attended ranged from fairly insignificant infringements of marital duties to the most disgraceful acts: the parties accused each other of adultery, drinking, beating, humiliations, insults, ill-treatment of children, sluttishness, venereal diseases, prostitution, sodomy, criminal offences (in particular thefts), falsifying of documents, incest. These examples could be multiplied, and the disgraceful behaviour of the parties was often described explicitly, omitting no confidential details, in the hostile atmosphere which I have presented above. It is not surprising that the spouse's hearing such charges against himself usually culminated, sometimes because of their direct influence irrespective of whether they were true or not, in a definite break in the common life: "having heard these lies I won't live with my wife any more" (T-150), "after what my husband said today I couldn't go back to him" (T-117) – these were words which I recorded in the courtroom.

In light of such accusations as these it would appear a demand should be made on the court to relax the tension between the spouses. Here, however, a serious antinomy appears. The less mutual fault-finding and tension, the greater the chance of bringing the parties to reconciliation, but, as I have said above, the more fault-finding and tension there is, the better the court is able to learn the degree of breakdown: determining this, and, in consequence, limiting divorce to instances of complete and permanent marital failure is contrary to the intention to bring the spouses to reconciliation. Therefore, when aiming at determining the degree of breakdown, the judge has to limit himself in restraining the accusation of the parties; to find a way of conducting the trial which best serves the contradictory legislative goals requires experience and moderation on his part. Nevertheless, despite this difficulty, the judge can always contribute to appeasement of conflict at least by means of a kind and lenient approach to the parties. This approach is the more desirable in that those who appear before the divorce court are usually in urgent need of kindness, especially from the judge. This came out clearly in the interviews of divorced and reconciled persons. All of them were asked to make "remarks concerning the course of the divorce suit", and 44 of them, i.e. about one third of the whole sample, spontaneously emphasized the kindness, tact, sympathy shown them by the court; and many of them spoke about the kindness of the judge in a manner indicating that it had been a real benefit to them: "I was surprised..., I had been so much afraid of the court, but then it appeared that it wasn't so dreadful, the atmosphere was very pleasant, the judge – kind, I saw that he sympathized with me" (D-60), "the atmosphere of the trial could not have been better, I had imagined it would be much worse, it was not so bad due to the judge's excellent behaviour" (D-122), "the judge and the laymen were full of sympathy, I cried... and the judge spoke to me so nicely" (D-26), "I was completely satisfied with the court, the judge was very just indeed, it was evident that he was very human and sympathized with me" (D-62), "the woman-judge was like a mother, I cried so much, and she called me 'dear child' and consoled me as best she could" (D-40), "the whole court smiled at me and encouraged me, I was moved" (D-104).

One should not, however, imagine that the attitude of the court is always friendly to the parties: it sometimes exhibits undeserved anger, impatience and jeering. There are only a few judges who behave in this unfriendly way: in particular those who are exhausted and nervous; and it seems, from long observation of their activity, that even they behave this way only sometimes, during periods of special tiredness, illness or other difficulties. This behaviour was clearly evident in 11 of 153 trials attended. Thus, in case T-150, the judge shouted at the defendant husband who did not know how to answer the question "who was guilty of the breakdown". In case D-139 he was angry because of the defendant wife's excitement: "don't gabble so quickly and so much"; in another case he said to the crying wife: "you should have cried in the course of your marriage, now this wiping of your eyes and nose is of no interest, it only disturbs us" (T-145). In some other cases the judge jeered at the parties. This behaviour was also mentioned in the interviews of divorcees: 12 of them, when answering the above mentioned question about the course of the divorce suit, complained of the unkindness or spitefulness of the judge: "the judge spoke brutally, impetuously, openly" (D-25); "he made malicious remarks, when I said that my husband had been unfaithful, he interrupted me and asked: 'and are you a saint? Did you never commit adultery?'... He didn't change his attitude until he realized that my husband was entirely guilty" (D-42); "the judge was unkind and vulgar, he spoke to me as to a criminal offender" (D-28); "even I, being the plaintiff, was treated like an accused, unkindly and very shortly..., one feels all the time as if one had stolen something" (D-119). It is probable that such behaviour on the part of the judges has an unfavourable effect upon relations between the spouses: for, each party has an understandable inclination to blame the other spouse for all the unpleasant experiences suffered in the course of the divorce suit.

The data collected in the interviews made it possible to learn the scope of the embittering influence of the above described behaviour of the parties, barristers, witnesses and judges. As I have said above, all the 131 divorcees were asked: "Did the divorce suit as such make relations between you and your partner more bitter than they had been before it began?" Those who answered that it had were subsequently asked to explain why. There were 31 subjects who said that it did. 14 of them believed that it was the very fact of filing the petition which had intensified the conflict; of these, 3 supposed that the further course of the suit had also had some aggravating influence. The remaining 17 emphasized only the aggravating influence of its further course. Thus, in all, 20 divorcees, i.e. 15.3 per cent of the whole sample, complained of the embittering impact of the further course of the trial. They gave various reasons for this. 11 of them gave as a reason the charges and fault-finding in the courtroom: "my husband lied, he slandered me..., the divorce suit just showed us how much we hated each other" (D-83), "my husband behaved in a superior manner, he jeered and laughed at me" (D-43), "we might possibly have been brought into harmony somehow, but in the course of the trial we began to disclose everything, and reconciliation appeared impossible" (D-125). 4 subjects gave as the reason for the aggravation of conflict the behaviour of barristers or witnesses: "the husband's barrister spoke roughly to me" (D-75), the barrister "used very unpleasant arguments, his behaviour was disgusting and tactless" (D-77), my wife "called witnesses whom I had never met before..., it would be difficult to tell how much she injured me" (D-66). One of the divorced women gave as the reason of aggravation of conflict, among other things, the behaviour of the judge who, according to her, did not create an atmosphere favourable to reconciliation: "it is the court which definitely breaks up the marriage", she said (D-125) [9]. Lastly, 7 subjects spoke about bad behaviour which had occurred out of court in the course of the trial, and, in their opinion, had been an effect of an aggravating influence of the suit, and simultaneously gave rise to the further embitterment: the husband "made scenes, I was beaten and ill-treated by him" (D-3), "there were unbelievable quarrels..., once I beat her..., she then went to the police and I was arrested..., there were quarrels every day, it was a hell of a life" (D-65), "my husband behaved properly in the courtroom..., but it would be difficult to put into words what he then did at home to revenge himself; I called the police in five times..., he destroyed my things, brought home prostitutes" (D-42).

It was not only divorcees who revealed the embittering influence of the divorce suit: I also asked all the judges and barristers interviewed about it. It is interesting that 22 out of 60 barristers, and as many as 28 out of 41 judges, found this influence to be particularly forceful: they said they had come across, some of them frequently, cases where the marriage could have been saved before the filing of the petition, but the suit aggravated the relations between the spouses to such a degree that the chance disappeared. The difference between the proportion of such views held by barristers and judges could possibly be explained by the fact that the irritating influence of the suit is more usually the effect of the barristers' behaviour than the judges'; some of the barristers interviewed may have believed that revealing they had ruined the chance of reconciliation in the suits they had conducted would bring them into disrepute, and probably did not give frank

[9] The behaviour of the court was here considered by the subject interviewed as one of the irritating factors; the mutual fault-finding was another factor, and that is why the same interview has been mentioned here for the second time.

answers. I then put some further questions to barristers and judges who had witnessed the losing of the chance of reconciliation, in order to learn which elements of the trial, in their opinion, have the most embittering influence. They mentioned chiefly the behaviour of the parties in and out of the courtroom, of the barristers, witnesses and judge; they also pointed out the influence of filing the petition.

3.2. *Conciliatory Activity*

3.2.1. The above remarks indicate that in the further course of the divorce suit the chance of reconciliation differs from that during the conciliatory session: new circumstances appear some of which increase, others decrease, the chance. Under these changing circumstances the court renews its efforts at conciliation. They are renewed as early as at the first sitting following the session; the majority of the judges start sitting with a new attempt to bring the parties into harmony. They hope that in cases where the filing of petition was the result of temporary excitement, the cooling-off period between the conciliatory session and the next sitting of the court may have helped in overcoming the conflict; this is, in particular, the belief of the hopeful judges: at the conciliatory session "I try to direct the parties properly, to furnish them with some material for reflection, then comes the adjournment..., and time to utilize the material...; I treat the conciliatory session as the initial part of the process of bringing about a reconciliation, the further efforts should be made... by the spouses themselves" (J-3).

Conciliation at the beginning of the next sitting is usually limited to a brief question: "has the attitude of the parties not changed since the conciliatory session?" (T-2), "have you not become reconciled" (T-123), "have you not changed your intention?" (T-66). There are also, however, more intense conciliatory efforts, made mainly by the hopeful judges.

3.2.2. In the further course of the divorce suit all the judges renewed attempts at conciliation. They did it in a way resembling their activity at the conciliatory session. When they saw real chance, the hopeful judges made serious efforts. The skeptical usually limited themselves to asking, at the very end of the suit, about the possibility of reconciliation. Some of them, however, increased their efforts, chiefly the one whose skeptical attitude was tabulated above in table 7: the evidence gathered gave him new conciliatory arguments. Among these were the situation of the children, state of health of the parties, their age, their previous affection, bad terms between the husband and his concubine. There were also some divorcees who, in the interviews, spoke of this change of attitude: at the conciliatory session the judge's "words were cool, it did not last more than a minute, and at the next sitting he spoke a great deal..., he attacked my wife saying she should return to me" (D-14); "the session lasted but 10 minutes, the judge asked only whether we definitely wanted divorce..., but at the next sitting he persuaded us, he said he would fix another date, and asked us to make one more attempt" (D-117); at the conciliatory session "I was discouraged by such a formal treatment..., there was no conciliation at all; it was followed by a lengthy interval", and then the judge appeared to be "a completely different man..., we were only then pressed to think it over and to become reconciled" (D-48).

4. EFFECTS OF CONCILIATION

4.1. *Effects of Conciliation in the Trials Attended*

The observation of trials did not yield many facts on final results of the court's conciliatory activity: the majority of the trials attended began in 1961 or 1962, and therefore it was too early to find out what the results were before concluding the present investigations. Some of the effects, however, came out clearly enough. Firstly it appeared that the conciliatory session, the chief means used to reconcile the parties, brings them to reconciliation only in exceptional cases. 80 of 84 sessions attended were ineffective. In 1 case the plaintiff withdrew the petition, but the withdrawal was the outcome of previous reconciliation which had taken place out of court. The remaining 3 sessions gave partial results. The parties, intending to make an attempt at reconciliation, asked the court to suspend the proceedings; however, two of the suspensions were followed by continuation of proceedings, and eventually resulted in pronouncement of divorce; and in 1 case only, conducted by the judge whom I have mentioned above as being particularly skilful in bringing on reconciliation, did the suspension last until the completion of collecting empirical data, i.e. 30 June 1963 [10]: this was the only case where suspension could have led to final discontinuation.

[10] See above, p. 13.

The figure for successful reconciliations grows in the further course of the trials. 2 of the 153 trials attended resulted in a withdrawal, and 1 of the withdrawals seemed to be, at least to some degree, an outcome of the conciliatory session and the parties' reflection during the subsequent cooling-off period; it is interesting that the session was conducted by the same skilful judge. A further 4 suits resulted in suspension; only in 1 of them was the suspension followed by continuation of proceedings; in the remaining 3 the suspension lasted till the empirical data had been collected and may eventually have resulted in final discontinuation. These 3 suspensions occurred under the evident influence of the judges' conciliatory efforts: these were those judges whose attitude I have classed above as hopeful.

The observation of divorce suits, although not showing clearly the effects of the court's conciliatory activity, seems to suggest that two facts appear with regularity. The first is that reconciliation more often comes about in the further course of the divorce suit than at the conciliatory session, even though the session had some influence in relaxing the conflict. The second, as one might have expected, is that the cases of reconciling the parties seem to be associated with activity of the hopeful judges: the five successes mentioned above took place in the suits conducted by them.

4.2. *Effects of Conciliation in the Trials Presented by Persons Interviewed*

The suits described by persons interviewed started in the first months of 1959: those of them which resulted in reconciliation were concluded early enough to learn of the final effect of conciliation; that is why the data derived from those suits are a particularly valuable source of information about the conciliatory activity of the court. As I have said in the initial part of the present study, there were among those trials 23 withdrawals and 9 suspensions of proceedings; 4 suspensions resulted in final discontinuance, 5 lasted till empirical data had been collected. 1 withdrawal and 2 suspensions were not, in the light of the court records, due to reconciliation: the plaintiff wife told the court she withdrew the petition not as result of reconciliation, but in order to avoid calling the incurably ill defendant to the court; and the suspensions were ordered by the court for procedural reasons. A further 12 withdrawals and 1 suspension occurred before the conciliatory session: thus, even if they had been an effect of reconciliation, the reconciliation was not due to the efforts of the judge; therefore those 13 cases were of no interest in the present investigations. On the other hand, the remaining 10 withdrawals and 6 suspensions occurred at the conciliatory session or later, and it was, in the light of the court records, quite possible that they were an outcome of reconciliation, and that reconciliation was caused by the efforts of the judge. To ascertain whether this had been the case and, moreover, whether the possible reconciliations appeared permanent, each of those 16 couples was interviewed. How the interviewing was done has been described above, and I have also mentioned that I succeeded in 13 out of 16 cases: 8 interviews were given by a spouse whose suit had resulted in withdrawal, 5 by a spouse whose suit had been suspended [11].

The first of the questions asked those 13 subjects were aimed at learning whether withdrawal or suspension had been as a result of reconciliation, and whether reconciliation had been due to the effort of the judge: every subject was asked whether he remembered the conciliatory session and whether the session decreased his wish to get a divorce, as well as the wish of his spouse. Then each of them was asked, "How did the judge try to bring you to reconciliation?". Lastly: "Did you become reconciled due to 1. persuasion of the judge at the conciliatory session?, 2. persuasion of the judge in the further course of the trial?, 3. what other circumstances?".

The answers given indicated that 3 subjects did not become reconciled at all, if reconciliation means at least an attempt at returning to the common life. One of them, the defendant husband whose wife asked the court to suspend the proceedings, did not know what her motives were: "Perhaps the family advised her to give up", but "we did not become reconciled..., I then met her once in the street..., she said that she did not care for me at all" (R-3). The defendant wife, who in case R-7 had contested divorce, did not know why her husband had withdrawn the petition; she only supposed that "perhaps he had no arguments and was advised by the barrister not to go on with the suit"; and she deplored there had been no reconciliation. Lastly, in case R-1, the plaintiff, who withdrew the petition at the conciliatory session, maintained firmly that the withdrawal had been a result of misunderstanding: "I didn't want it at all, I absolutely didn't intend to live with her..., I arrived late at the session..., the judge muttered something, I didn't quite follow him, I nodded and said 'yes' or 'no', I don't remember

[11] See pp. 17-18.

which, and that was all..., I knew less on leaving the courtroom than on the arrival... My barrister was absent, I was told by him later that the judge had asked me whether I would like to become reconciled and I had answered 'yes'. Nothing has changed since then..., it was not reconciliation, but my foolishness".

The remaining 10 subjects interviewed said that the withdrawal or suspension was connected with reconciliation: the parties returned or at least attempted to return to a common life. However, in the opinion of 5 of them the reconciliation was definitely not an outcome of the judge's efforts. It was a result of the circumstances which had occurred out of the court: "The judge did not induce us to become reconciled..., my husband promised to improve, I believed he would change, I wanted to keep the parental home for my daughters" (R-2); the judge "did not induce us to become reconciled at all", the husband "declared he was against divorce because his mistress led him an awful life" (R-10); "the judge did not reconcile us at all..., my husband's mistress had left him..., that was why he had no more use for divorce" (R-9); "the judge was a formalist, we became reconciled, but it absolutely wasn't due to him", it was the result of the woman interviewed having a serious heart disease and an operation (R-4); at the session "the judge did not exert himself..., I was under the impression he was dealing with a thing, not human beings", reconciliation "was initiated by my husband who came to me, to my lodgings..., I felt sorry for him" (R-12).

In contradistinction to the here mentioned 5 subjects, the remaining 5 said in the interview that the conciliatory session had checked their or their partners' will to obtain a divorce, and that reconciliation had come about due to persuasion from the judge. They gave a detailed account of the judge's conciliatory efforts. "The judge... was simply wonderful, he spoke to us like a father" – said the subject in the above mentioned case R-8 [12]; – "if there were more such judges, many a divorce would probably be avoided... This judge showed us so much tolerance and warmth..., our case is the best example of how much can be done by a good judge". Also in the case R-13 the judge spoke so "that it relieved my great excitement, and my husband's as well", although it was the barrister's efforts which mainly contributed to reconciliation. Another woman, reconciled due to the persuasion of the judge, had filed petition not to obtain divorce, but to "frighten the husband with the possibility of divorce" and to come to reconciliation

[12] On p. 93.

in the court: a carefully conducted conciliatory session, "after which a period for reflection was given..., induced my husband to meet me half-way, and he promised to improve" (R-6). In case R-11 the judge "made a great effort" to bring the parties to reconciliation, and influenced not only the plaintiff husband, but, moreover, soothed the offended pride of the wife who, in fact, did not want a divorce, but also did not want "to hold out her hand first". A similar appeasement was reported by the plaintiff wife in interview R-5 given together with her husband [13]: "my feelings were hurt by the fact of my husband's filing the petition, and that was why I consented to divorce..., the judge analysed the causes, he found them insignificant..., he spoke in a very convincing manner"; there was also "the seldomness of the court sittings which enabled me to think the whole matter out". In the interval between the sittings "we met" – added the husband, – "we had a long conversation, and decided to make an attempt".

Thus 10 of the 13 couples interviewed became reconciled, of which only 5 under the influence of the court. In the light of the above remarks it is, however, far from being clear whether improvement appeared permanent: an important issue from the point of view of the real value of reconciliation. To learn its permanency those reconciled were asked some further questions. The first of them was: "Do you think that you will never stand before the divorce court again?", and "Does your husband (wife) share this view?"; then there came two further questions: "Do you regret reconciliation?", and "In your opinion does your husband (wife) regret reconciliation?".

The answers incline one to divide the 10 cases of reconciliation once again. 4 persons reconciled – of which as many as 3 ascribed reconciliation to the efforts of the judge – live with their spouses, find reconciliation to be permanent, and do not believe their marriage will ever be dissolved by divorce: "We will never divorce, now everything is all right" (R-5); "I rather think not, now my husband is doing his best..., I also take care to avoid any trouble at home" (R-13); "My husband is wonderful, we are both as much in love as on our honeymoon..., I am so happy I have not left him; it was simply necessary to mature and to suffer a bit in order to appreciate what one has" (R-8); the husband "is already retired, he has no money and that is why he will remain with me in old age..., I don't regret reconciliation..., he possibly is even better to me than I am to him..., but it won't be a real marriage any more..., I shall never trust him" (R-9).

[13] This interview was mentioned above, p. 18.

On the other hand the remaining 6 persons reconciled – of which one reconciled due to the effort of the judge – disclosed the very poor state of their unions: "I regret reconciliation, my husband continues drinking and hardly anything has changed" (R-11); "My husband promised to improve, he returned home, but a few days later... he moved to his mistress again" (R-6); "I would have done better to divorce him..., cohabitation with my husband is horrible, anything would be better than the present state of affairs" (R-12); "He is a stranger to me..., he does not think of coming back to me either..., I certainly shall obtain a divorce" (R-4); "I will file a new petition before long..., my husband urgently wants me to do it, I very much regret reconciliation, otherwise I would have had all that behind me, and now I go through the strain once again" (R-2). The last 2 women think they certainly will, the former 4 that they possibly will, stand before the divorce court again. Those of them who will, face a second divorce suit; reconciliation will have resulted in further hardship.

The sample of those reconciled described here is small and it was taken from the district of the Cracow Court only. Its enlargement appeared impracticable: I had no means of interviewing the persons reconciled in the other courts, and only the reconciled spouses, not judges nor barristers, can give information about effectiveness and permanency of reconciliation. Especially the barristers, asked about the further life of the reconciled spouses, were unable to furnish any information: their contact with clients ends, in principle, at the moment the suit is concluded. Their answers were useful in one point only. I asked all 60 about the causes of reconciliation; and, in particular, whether reconciliations known to them were due mainly to the activity of the court, to the fact that sometimes neither party really wants divorce, or to any other reasons. Only 26 barristers answered the question; the others did not know how to answer or had never met with reconciliation. The majority of those who answered – as many as 16 – did not consider the activity of the court to be of any importance; they mentioned, among the factors of import, their own persuasion, change in the parties' circumstances of life, lack of a real wish to obtain divorce. On the other hand the remaining 10 barristers considered the efforts of the court a factor contributing to reconciliations in the suits conducted by them. The barristers' opinions seem to confirm the data collected in the interviews with those who became reconciled: a considerable proportion of reconciliations take place independently of the judge.

The information furnished by reconciled persons, though limited, seems to contribute to an appraisal of the effectiveness of conciliatory proceedings. As I have said above, its effectiveness had become a matter of divergent conjectures. According to the figures drawn from the Ministry of Justice, its effectiveness is high, since 3.4 – 4.0 per cent of the finally concluded divorce cases result in reconciliation. In the light of the above presented factual data this conjecture seems to be dubious. It is true that in my sample also it seemed, at first sight, that there were 13 cases where, due to the activity of the court, the parties had been brought to reconciliation. However, in 3 of them reconciliation did not take place. The majority of the reconciled unions were not reconciled permanently, and half of them reached a reconciliation without any influence on the part of the court; this latter finding has been confirmed by information furnished by barristers. Only 3 of the couples interviewed became reconciled permanently and under the influence of the court: this means 1.4 per cent of all the finally concluded suits contained in my sample. This figure is suitable for a cautious comparison with the proportion of reconciliations drawn from the statistics of the Ministry of Justice: cautious, because the data of the Ministry concern the suits concluded in the year which was a basis for calculation, and my sample was taken from the suits filed in the year which I chose as a basis for my inquiry. Nevertheless, the comparison seems to be justified, since the data of the Ministry have, like my data, been derived from the period 1959-1962, and during that period neither the figures of finally concluded divorce suits nor figures of reconciliations changed to any considerable degree in Poland. The comparison indicates that the conciliatory activity of the divorce court is far from being so effective as one might expect when studying the official statistical data. Nevertheless its effects – the number of those permanent reconciliations which come about due to the efforts of the court – should not be underestimated: they certainly are much more valuable than is believed by the legal writers mentioned above who simply deny that this activity is of any value at all.

VI

RECRIMINATION *

1. GOALS AND CONJECTURES

1.1. The principle of breakdown has been, in the majority of those countries which accept it, seriously limited by the rule of recrimination: a provision preventing the spouse solely guilty of breakdown from claiming divorce [1]. This provision is a consequence of a broader and long established maxim: "nemo turpitudinem suam allegans audiatur", no one who alleges his own guilt can be heard; the maxim is regarded as expressing disapproval of gaining from one's own wrongdoing, and as an important means of motivation: being at the disposal of those who are guilty, the law would not restrain people from blameworthy behaviour.

However broadly adopted, the rule of recrimination is not necessarily associated with the acceptance of the breakdown of marriage as a ground for divorce: it is unknown to the laws of Czechoslovakia [2], Roumania and Eastern Germany and there are strong tendencies to discard it in the Scandinavian legal systems [3], where breakdown of marriage is, subject to elapse of some period of separation, one of the grounds for divorce. Among East European legislations it has thus far been adopted by the family law of Bulgaria [4], and in the Soviet Union its acceptance was due rather to the decrees of the Supreme Court than to the contents of any particular statutory provision [5]. In Western Europe this rule is known, *inter alia,* to the Swiss [6], Austrian [7] and

* Some parts of this chapter appeared in the *American Journal of Comparative Law* (1966/4), p. 603 *et seq.*

[1] The word 'recrimination' is used here in a meaning which differs from that in use in the English legal language. In the United States and in Britain, where until quite recently matrimonial offences of either spouse constituted the main grounds for divorce, and the general principle of breakdown of marriage was unknown, the doctrine of recrimination required that the plaintiff in a divorce suit be innocent of the matrimonial offence justifying the petition.

[2] This rule was, however, accepted by Para. more s. and 4 of the Czechoslovakian Family Law of 1949 which was in force until 1964.

[3] W. Müller-Freienfels, *Ehe und Recht* (1962), p. 145 *et seq.*

[4] Art. 47 s. 2 of the Bulgarian Law of Persons and the Family.

[5] Cf. the decrees mentioned by G. M. Svierdlov in *Sovietskoje siemiejnoje pravo (Soviet Family Law)* (1951) pp. 92, 93.

[6] Art. 142 s. 2 of the Swiss Civil Code.

[7] Para. 55 s. 2 of the Law of Marriage.

West-German [8] family laws. However, the majority of the law-makers who advocate it find it too hard to enforce without any limits. Hence exceptions to the rule: some legislations allow the court to decree divorce at request of the guilty spouse if the innocent partner agrees to divorce [9] or does not oppose its pronouncement [10]; moreover, refusal of consent or opposition are not always effective: even in the face of opposition the Austrian court shall decree divorce if, in the light of the commonly accepted customs, the continuance of a given marriage is not justified [11], the West-German court – if the spouse who opposes divorce does not intend to continue cohabitation [12], the Bulgarian court – if pronouncement of divorce is indicated by important social reasons [13]. Only a few legislators, among them the Swiss, introduced the rule of recrimination without limits.

The Polish family law, following the former norms, in particular the Law of Marriage of 1945 and the numerous decrees of the Supreme Court which had been pronounced on its ground, introduced the rule of recrimination first in Art. 30 of the Family Code of 1950, and then in Art. 56 Para. 3 of the present Family and Guardianship Code. As I have mentioned above, according to both these provisions, divorce cannot, in principle, be pronounced, "if the petitioner alone was guilty of breakdown".

1.2. The goals which the legislators intended to achieve when introducing the rule of recrimination can be deduced from decisions of the Supreme Court, as well as from declarations of certain legal writers, in particular of those who joined the legislative bodies and, consequently, influenced the contents of the legal provisions. These are complex aims, and similar to those which have traditionally been attributed to the principle "nemo turpitudinem suam allegans audiatur". The first of them is the adjustment of divorce law to morality: according to the guide lines pronounced in 1952 by the Supreme Court [14], the legislators eliminated, in principle, pronouncement of divorce at request of the solely guilty spouse, in order to act "against infringement of socialist mor-

[8] Para. 48 s. 2 of the Law of Marriage.
[9] Art. 47 s. 2 of the Bulgarian Law of Persons and the Family.
[10] Para. 48 s. 2 of the West-German Law of Marriage, Para. 55 s. 2 of the Austrian Law of Marriage.
[11] Para. 55 s. 2 of the Law of Marriage.
[12] Para. 48 s. 2 of the Law of Marriage.
[13] Art. 47 s. 2 of the Law of Persons and the Family.
[14] On the meaning of the guide lines see above, p. 25, footnote 3.

ality" [15]. This purpose has also been pointed out in numerous decrees of the Supreme Court [16]. The guide lines, as well as the decrees, indicate that by "infringement of socialist morality" the Supreme Court means the violating of the "moral feelings of working masses" [17] or, more broadly, of the "moral opinion of the community" [18]: thus the enforcement of the rule of recrimination would be in line with a commonly accepted moral demand, and the legal provisions which I am talking about were introduced to meet it.

The educative purposes of these provisions have also been emphasized. The Supreme Court and certain legal writers assumed here two hypotheses. According to the first, the spouse inclined to commit a breach of marital duties will be prevented from it by awareness that, if the breach resulted in breakdown of marriage, he would not be allowed to request divorce. According to the second, enabling the solely guilty spouse to claim divorce would induce people to intentional breach of marital duties in order to cause the breakdown of marriage, and, subsequently, to get a divorce. Both these views have been expressed more than once. The guide lines mentioned above asserted that the rule of recrimination should "counteract the danger of marital break-ups", and "play an educative and restraining role with respect to those spouses whose social maturity and moral standards are too low to prevent them from... an irresponsible approach to their own duties; and numerous decrees of the Supreme Court emphasize that the admission of divorce "at request of the spouse solely guilty of the breakdown... would, from the psychological point of view, encourage the breaking of marital unions" [19]: the spouse "inclined to shirk his responsibilities... would intentionally cause the breakdown of marriage... (usually by entering into connections with another woman...), and after some time would request divorce, founding his claim on his own fault"; moreover, after divorce "he could marry again, and once more behave in the same way" [20]. Similar reasons were pointed out by various legal writers: in their opinion the admission of divorce at request of the solely guilty

[15] Resolution of the whole Civil Chamber of the Supreme Court of 26 April, 1952, C. Prez. 798/51.

[16] Cf. in particular, decrees: of 13 November 1946, C. III 639/46; of 20 November 1952, C.600/52; of 20 January 1953, C.2244/52; of 4 July 1958, 4 CR.1016/57; of 26 May 1959, 1 CR.632/57.

[17] Decree of 20 January, 1953, C.2244/52.

[18] Decree of 14 May, 1955, 1 CR.746/55.

[19] Decree of 28 May, 1948, WaC 126/48.

[20] Decree of 15 February, 1947, C.III 913/46. The same idea was contained in decrees: of 13 November, 1946, C.III 639/46; of 10 March 1951, C.48/51; of 4 July, 1958, 4 CR.1016/57.

spouse "would not restrain from, but simply encourage to infringement of duties of husband and wife" [21].

2. RECRIMINATION AND THE SOCIALIST MORALITY

Does the rule of recrimination, formulated as I have presented it above, lead to the achievement of the purposes mentioned? The first of them is to meet a commonly accepted moral demand, and, consequently, to adjust legal provisions to morality. Thus, in the light of the present investigations, the enforcement of the rule of recrimination does not seem to be a commonly accepted demand in Poland. The point was offered for consideration, by the Public Opinion Research Centre, to the above mentioned sample of 2355 respondents from all over the country. Each of them was asked whether, and under what conditions, the law should allow the spouse solely responsible for the breakdown of marriage to claim divorce. Table 8 provides the distribution of answers.

TABLE 8

Opinions on the Rule of Recrimination

Item No.	Answers	Number of subjects	%
1	The guilty spouse should be prevented from claiming divorce without the adversary's consent	787	33.4
2	The guilty spouse should be allowed to claim divorce regardless of his (her) fault	702	29.8
3	I oppose divorce in general	358	15.2
4	I don't know	486	20.7
5	No answer	22	0.9
	TOTALS	2355	100.0

As follows from this table, only 63.2 per cent of the persons interviewed answered the question, the rest had no clear opinion, gave no answer or in general opposed divorce. From among these 63.2 per cent, somewhat over a half (33.4 per cent of all the subjects) were for, almost a half (29.8 per cent of all the subjects) were against recrimination despite the limiting of recrimination by the innocent defendant's consent. In the light of these figures it seems that, contrary to the legislators' belief, the enforcement of the recrimination rule is far from being a generally accepted moral principle in Poland.

[21] J. Gwiazdomorski, M. Grudzinski, S. Kaleta, A. Wolter, *op. cit.*, p. 65.

TABLE 9

Opinions on the Rule of Recrimination and the Socio-Professional Status of Respondents

Answers as in Table 8	Socio-Professional Status of Respondents							
	Farmer (small land -owner)	Farm worker, forestry worker, member of rural co-operative	Un-skilled worker	Skilled worker	Artisan	White -collar	Other profession	Occupation unknown
Answer 1	274 (35.4 %)	11 (31.4 %)	42 (26.1 %)	155 (32.0 %)	27 (27.0 %)	245 (34.4 %)	7 (29.2 %)	26 (40.0 %)
Answer 2	186 (24.0 %)	11 (31.4 %)	53 (32.9 %)	159 (32.9 %)	32 (32.0 %)	244 (34.3 %)	7 (29.2 %)	10 (15.4 %)
Answer 3	156 (20.2 %)	5 (14.3 %)	25 (15.5 %)	61 (12.6 %)	14 (14.0 %)	83 (11.6 %)	4 (16.6 %)	10 (15.4 %)
Answer 4	149 (19.2 %)	8 (22.9 %)	40 (24.9 %)	104 (21.5 %)	27 (27.0 %)	134 (18.8 %)	6 (25.0 %)	18 (27.7 %)
Answer 5	9 (1.2 %)	—	1 (0.6 %)	5 (1.0 %)	—	6 (0.9 %)	—	1 (1.5 %)
TOTALS	774 (100.0 %)	35 (100.0 %)	161 (100.0 %)	484 (100.0 %)	100 (100.0 %)	712 (100.0 %)	24 (100.0 %)	65 (100.0 %)

TABLE 10

Opinions on the Rule of Recrimination and the Education of Respondents

Answers as in Table 8	Education of Respondents						
	Un-completed elementary	Elemen-tary	Un-completed secondary	Secondary	Un-completed higher	Higher	Un-defined
Answer 1	146 (34.4 %)	272 (32.1 %)	148 (34.6 %)	160 (34.9 %)	31 (29.2 %)	27 (31.8 %)	3 (50.0 %)
Answer 2	80 (18.9 %)	242 (28.6 %)	144 (33.6 %)	159 (34.6 %)	44 (41.6 %)	32 (37.6 %)	1 (16.7 %)
Answer 3	118 (27.8 %)	129 (15.2 %)	51 (11.9 %)	41 (8.9 %)	12 (11.3 %)	5 (5.9 %)	2 (33.3 %)
Answer 4	73 (17.2 %)	198 (23.4 %)	83 (19.4 %)	93 (20.3 %)	19 (17.9 %)	20 (23.5 %)	—
Answer 5	7 (1.7 %)	6 (0.7 %)	2 (0.5 %)	6 (1.3 %)	—	1 (1.2 %)	—
TOTALS	424 (100.0 %)	847 (100.0 %)	828 (100.0 %)	459 (100.0 %)	106 (100.0 %)	85 (100.0 %)	6 (100.0 %)

The tables 9 and 10 present the degree to which the collected opinions depend upon socio-professional status and education of subjects interviewed.

Thus the rule of recrimination is the less often proposed the higher the level of education of respondents. Its acceptance is more frequent in rural areas: 35.4 per cent of all the small landowners interviewed were for, and only 24.0 per cent were against it; and the high figure of those in its favour seems to be not only the effect of the lower educational status of rural people, but also an outcome of some milder form of the traditional anti-divorce attitude, characteristic of the countryside. On the other hand, the workers – i.e. the group of people whose views the legislator would probably be inclined to recognise as the main source of the rules of socialist morality – have a different approach: among the 59.0 per cent of unskilled, and 64.9 per cent of skilled workers who answered the above question, the majority declared against recrimination.

The answers obtained through the Public Opinion Research Centre questionnaire did not disclose the reasons for the subjects being for or against recrimination. To ascertain the reasons, and in particular to find out whether all those in favour of recrimination were influenced by moral motives, was important to the present considerations. I therefore tried to ask the respondents of the Public Opinion Research Centre about the reasons. However, it appeared in the pilot study that questions concerning reasons were too difficult for the average respondent, and therefore they had to be dropped. To answer them I interviewed an additional sample, not only educated better than average, but also composed of subjects to whom I could explain the meaning of each question. The sample was composed of 323 evening students of law at the University of Cracow who, in 1963, answered a questionnaire given and explained to them in a lecture. I intentionally chose the evening students, because they are older than the fulltime students and had more experience, especially in the matters dealt with in the questionnaire; hence, the probability of better considered answers.

The first of the questions put to the students was: "Should the spouse solely guilty of breakdown of marriage (e.g. because of adultery, cruelty, etc.) be: (a) prevented from claiming divorce without his innocent partner's consent? (b) allowed to claim divorce equally with the innocent partner?". 32 students did not make any choice: they had no clear opinion or, opposing divorce in general, refused to answer the question. 150 students declared for recrimination, some of them – for recrimination with limitations in exceptional cases. 141 students declared against recrimination. Two further questions were subsequently put to those for recrimination. First, an open-ended question: "Why?"; and afterwards three yes-and-no questions: "Do you think, in particular, that (a) it would be immoral to enable the guilty spouse to claim divorce against his innocent partner's will? (b) the guilty spouse should be punished? (c) everybody should know that if he is guilty, he won't easily get divorce?". These questions were aimed at finding out whether those in favour of recrimination were always guided by moral reasons. It seemed that if this was not the case, two other intentions might predominantly influence them. First, the wish to punish the guilty spouse. Secondly, the tendency towards an educative influence, closely connected with the legislator's aim described above: if an individual knew that he would not get a divorce if the fault were his own, the figure for breach of marital duties would decrease.

The answers obtained confirmed this guess. All the 150 in favour of recrimination accepted at least one of the yes-and-no questions. A considerable number of them answered the open-ended question as well. However, the majority of answers to the open-ended question contained just an explanation of the affirmative answer to the yes-and-no one. Only a few answers to the open-ended question revealed motives not mentioned in the yes-and-no questions: the wish to protect the innocent spouse and children from financial or other difficulties, the wish to make it impossible for the solely guilty spouse to contract a new marriage in which "he would do the same again" (ST-236), the care for "authority and dignity of the marriage union" (ST-244). When answering the yes-and-no questions, 117 (i.e. 78.0 per cent) of those for recrimination justified the tendency to its acceptance on moral grounds only (30 subjects) or in conjunction with some other motives (87 subjects). On the other hand, the remaining 33 (i.e. 22.0 per cent) declared for recrimination not because of its rejection being immoral: they aimed at punishing the solely guilty spouse, at making it generally known that if a spouse is solely guilty he will not get a divorce easily, or at achieving other purposes mentioned in answers to the open-ended question.

The data collected by the Public Opinion Research Centre prove that there does not exist in Poland any common demand for accepting the rule of recrimination; and the information furnished by evening students throws more light on these data. Namely, it appeared that, in the student sample, 22.0 per cent of those in favour of the rule were not stimulated by any moral reasons. It is clear that the students interviewed – mainly white collar workers of southern Poland, completing their education – do not represent the opinion of the country's whole population. Therefore one does not know whether, in a more representative sample, the proportion of those for recrimination motivated by non-moral reasons would be the same; it seems, however, to be sure that a certain number of them would appear. This leads to an interesting conclusion: the enforcement of recrimination is not only far from being a common demand in Poland, but, even for its advocates, it is not necessarily a demand of a moral nature.

3. RECRIMINATION AS A MOTIVE OF HUMAN BEHAVIOUR

The educative impact of the rule of recrimination is, as I have said above, another legislative purpose of import. According to hypotheses widespread in decisions of the Supreme Court and in legal literature, the enforcement of the rule restrains people from two kinds of reprehensible behaviour: from rash and irresponsible approach to the duties of husband and wife, and from intentional annihilating of marital life in order to obtain divorce. If these hypotheses were true, the discarding of recrimination from a given legal system would result in an increase in marital failures, and, consequently, in the divorce rate. To test these hypotheses properly, one should divide the population of Poland into two comparable parts, and to subject one of them to provisions containing the rule of recrimination, and the other to identical provisions, but without the rule: if the divorce rate were significantly higher in the second group, the hypotheses, or at least one of them, would be verified. It is clear that such an experiment cannot be made. However, certain experiences in foreign countries, in particular in Finland, are here of some use. In Finland the breakdown of marriage is one of several grounds for divorce, among others being the widely accepted grounds of adultery, cruelty, desertion. Until 1948 the rule of recrimination was in force in Finland: in a case in which the breakdown of marriage was the ground for divorce, the predominantly guilty spouse was prevented from claiming divorce. This rule was discarded in 1948 [22]. However, its cessation, in the years 1948-1957, did not result in any significant rise in the divorce rate, in any significant shifts in the number of petitions on the ground of breakdown of marriage and on other grounds [23]: these data suggest that, at least in Finland, the rule of recrimination was not an effective motivation for human behaviour.

[22] See Art. 69a of the Finnish Marriage Law of 1948.

[23] Snaevarr, Verhandlungen des 21. Nordischen Juristentages, Helsingfors, 1957, 1959, Suppl. I, p. 32 (quoted after W. Müller-Freienfels, *op. cit.*, p. 147).

To test its effectiveness in Poland another means could also be used: that of asking people whether it restrained them, as well as those in their milieu, from breach of marital duties. Therefore I asked a sample of respondents: "In your opinion, does the rule denying the solely guilty spouse the right to claim divorce prevent husband and wife failing in their duties to each other?". The question was impersonal, but I expected that the answers would reflect experiences of the subjects interviewed, and of those with whom they were acquainted. Therefore the obtaining of answers from a sample representative for the whole country would possibly throw a good deal of light on the educative effectiveness of recrimination.

Unfortunately, the interviewing of such a sample appeared impossible for two reasons. First, the question could be sensibly addressed only to those who had previously known the rule of recrimination, because only their behaviour could have been influenced by the rule. Secondly – only to those who were able to follow its meaning, and to realise what their own motives of behaviour and those of their milieu really were. It is clear that the majority of the Public Opinion Research Centre repondents did not fulfil these two requirements either. Therefore I put the question only to the evening student sample, and, in addition, to the judges and barristers interviewed: I assumed that the fact of recrimination being in force was known not only to judges and barristers, but also to students of law. Table 11 presents information furnished by the students.

The table indicates that 70.6 per cent of those who answered the

TABLE 11

Opinion of the Evening Student Sample on the Educative Effectiveness of Recrimination

Question	Answers	Respondents who are or were married	Respondents who have never been married	TOTALS
In your opinion, does the rule denying the solely guilty spouse the right to claim divorce prevent husband and wife failing in their duties to each other?	yes	46 (21.8 %)	34 (30.4 %)	80 (24.8 %)
	no	155 (73.5 %)	73 (65.2 %)	228 (70.6 %)
	don't know	10 (4.7 %)	5 (4.4 %)	15 (4.6 %)
	TOTALS	211 (100.0 %)	112 (100.0 %)	323 (100.0 %)

question would not be restrained from infringement of marital duties by the rule of recrimination. This proportion becomes insignificantly higher if one takes into account only the answers of the 201 subjects who had had experience of marital life: married, widowed, divorced, i.e. of those respondents whose answers are of particular value because they probably reflect, at least to some degree, their own experiences, and not only conjectures concerning the feelings of the other people.

The judges and barristers interviewed also denied, and even more emphatically, the educative effectiveness of recrimination. Table 12 shows their answers.

TABLE 12

Opinion of Judges and Barristers on the Educative Effectiveness of Recrimination

Question	Answers	Judges	Barristers	TOTALS
In your opinion, does the rule denying the solely guilty spouse the right to claim divorce prevent husband and wife failing in their duties to each other?	yes	4 (9.8 %)	3 (5.0 %)	7 (6.9 %)
	no	33 (80.5 %)	53 (88.3 %)	86 (85.2 %)
	don't know	4 (9.7 %)	4 (6.7 %)	8 (7.9 %)
	TOTALS	41 (100.0 %)	60 (100.0 %)	101 (100.0 %)

These figures indicate that, in the opinion of 80.5 per cent of the judges and 88.3 per cent of the barristers interviewed, the rule of recrimination did not have preventive influence. Their answers were most decided, they frequently said: "absolutely not", "certainly not", and their replies were often accompanied by laughter which meant: "how could anybody believe in its restraining effect?". Only seven of them spoke with some hesitation: "probably not", "rather not". On the other hand, the answers of the few subjects who believed in the restraining effect were not unqualified: they maintained that the rule of recrimination restrains only "now and then" or "to a slight degree".

If the information furnished by students, judges and barristers were an accurate reflection of the views of the whole community, it might be concluded that the educative effect of recrimination in Poland is poor. However, it does not reflect these views accurately, and not only because the samples interviewed are not representative of the whole population of the country. The student answers were obtained by means of filling in a questionnaire, and, despite my scrupulous preliminary explanation, I was not quite certain whether, because of the difficulty of the question, all the answers were given after due consideration. The answers of the 107 students who had no experience of marital life were merely conjectures. The answers of the remaining 201 students might possibly be of more value; however, those of them who, not having had experience of marital conflicts, had never been inclined to commit a breach of conjugal duties, had had no chance of learning whether the danger of dismissal in a divorce suit restrained them from encroachments. The judges and barristers interviewed were more familiar with the problem because of frequent contact with the experiences of those involved in marital difficulties; this was particularly true in the case of barristers, due to their closer insight into the motives of their clients. However, one could not rely safely even on their answers: they are usually in touch with those whom the rule of recrimination did not restrain from failing in marital duties; and the spouses who have been restrained, if there are any, do not come to the barrister's office, and still less to the courtroom.

Thus the investigations on the educative impact of recrimination do not lead to a definite conclusion. They seem at most to justify a cautious assumption that the impact is insignificant, and the Finnish experience supports the point. If this assumption is true, it could easily be explained by the circumstances mentioned in several interviews with judges, barristers, and those students who did not limit themselves to a simple reply to a yes-and-no question. The first of these is poor knowledge of legal provisions: only a few know that the rule of recrimination is in force. The second, frequently emphasized, is the spontaneousness of behaviour of the spouses who infringe marital duties: those who commit adultery or are cruel, are governed by emotions and do not think about their procedural position in a possible divorce suit; it would be even more difficult to assume that, if recrimination were discarded, people would fail in their duties not because of emotions, but deliberately, to cause the breakdown of a working marriage in order to obtain divorce.

4. THE MORAL VALUE OF RECRIMINATION

The above considerations indicate that the rule of recrimination has not been commonly accepted, and that it probably is not an effective motivation for human behaviour. But this does not necessarily mean that it should be rejected: the fact that a moral rule has not been commonly accepted does not imply that it is not a good moral rule, and one deserving approval.

Those in favour of rejecting it are advocates of an uncompromising enforcement of the breakdown principle: they point out that, if a marriage has completely broken down, its dissolution should be made possible regardless of who is guilty of breakdown. For, how can one insist on dismissal of a petition only for the reason that it has been filed by the solely guilty spouse, if dismissal would not restore the broken consortium, and, consequently, would not improve the innocent partner's situation? Would the dismissal be a punishment for causing marital failure? What would be the use of it to the innocent spouse? It seems that it would be of no use, because dissolution of an unhappy marriage is a benefit for both spouses, the innocent included. Some go so far as to assert that the rule of recrimination makes no sense at all, because unilateral guilt in broken marriages hardly ever occurs.

The information gathered in interviews of 323 evening students indicates how common these opinions are. As I have said above, 141 of them were against recrimination. To these 141 I put an open-ended question "Why?", and, subsequently, two yes-and-no questions: "Do you think, in particular, that (a) if a marriage is a complete failure, its dissolution should be possible, irrespective of who is the guilty party? (b) unilateral guilt cannot be said to exist at all in unsuccessful marriages?".

In their answers, 140 of the 141 against recrimination accepted at least one of the yes-and-no questions: the first of them was accepted by 124, the second by 69 subjects. 42 subjects, not limiting themselves to this, also answered the open-ended question, and one subject answered only the open-ended question. Almost all the answers to the open-ended question contained merely reasons for an affirmative answer to the first of the yes-and-no questions. Among the reasons which frequently appeared was the opinion that "prohibition of divorce does not restore conjugal life" (ST-14), that "marriage cannot be made a punishment" (ST-57), that "social reasons, and in particular the welfare of children, point to the advisability of dissolving broken marriages irrespective of who is guilty" (ST-153). Several subjects emphasized the welfare of the innocent spouse: "single life is better than a common life with a bad partner" (ST-184), and dismissal of a divorce suit, even if desired by the innocent spouse, "would expose him to severe suffering" (ST-301).

Many subjects pointed out that welfare of both spouses requires dissolution of a broken marriage irrespective of the problem of guilt; the others were inclined to assist the solely guilty spouse "in the name of... the right of every human being to start his life anew" (ST-169).

Not all these arguments deserve approval, and in particular the opinion that unilateral guilt for marital failure does not occur: if the husband, unprovoked by his wife's conduct, treats her sadistically, if he conceals his criminal past from her before marriage or, after marriage, commits a criminal offence, it is only he who is guilty of the breakdown resulting from this behaviour. Nevertheless, in the light of the present investigations, some of the arguments used against recrimination seem to be justified. Among them, in particular, is the necessity of considering the interests of the solely guilty spouse, who sometimes also deserves protection: it clearly appeared in the courtroom how disastrous his position frequently is, how much he suffers because of marital conflict and the divorce suit, to what extent his own blameworthy behaviour had been determined by his background, education and past, i.e. the circumstances which, though in the eye of criminal law do not exempt from guilt and penalty, do, however, in a divorce trial, incline rather to assistance than to punishment by dismissal. Thus a plaintiff whose brutality, stupidity and quarrelsome temper gave rise to marital failure deserted his wife three years before the filing of the divorce suit, and one year before its filing entered into concubinage. His own and the witnesses' evidence indicate what factors had influenced his character: he lost his parents in early childhood, was subsequently deprived, by his foster mother and her husband, of assets left by his mother, was "very severely brought up" by them and beaten despite prolonged illness, so that he "tried to run away from them"; it was they who tried to make him marry in order to get him out of the house and to take his property (T-111). Similarly – in the case T-90, where breakdown of marriage had been mainly caused by the excessive niggardliness and despotic temper of the plaintiff, who told the court: "my mother died when I was 16, I was very strictly brought up and frequently beaten; there was always poverty and every penny was counted in the house in which I was reared, and in consequence I have counted every penny as well". In another suit, brought for the second time and having continued for a year and a half, the plaintiff said, crying, that, because of the pain caused by the marital failure and divorce trial, he had become completely broken: "I am unable to work, have no means of support, am hungry, and I simply cannot endure any more" (T-134); and in interview D-45 a deserted wife spoke about her husband's suffering resulting from the conflict between the old loyalty and new affection, making him "broken and unhappy".

So much for the factual data speaking against the rule of recrimination. However, the present investigations also resulted in collecting numerous data speaking strongly in favour of this rule. It appeared that its discarding would lead, at least in some situations, to morally unjustifiable effects. These are the situations in which the wrong done by the solely guilty spouse to his partner has been particularly blameworthy and painful. About twenty such situations appeared in the course of observation of trials and interviewing of divorcees, and in half of them a characteristic state of matters regularly emerged: the husband, after getting married, was completing his education for a lengthy period of time, and his wife, in order to assist him, worked to support the whole family. Subsequently, after getting a new job and standing, he deserted her, tired out by prolonged effort, for another, younger woman. Thus, in the case T-4 the defendant wife, in order to enable the plaintiff to continue academic studies, had for years maintained the whole family consisting of the spouses and two children, and her efforts and self-sacrifice were accurately described by numerous and trustworthy witnesses. The plaintiff had exploited her help, and, after having graduated and gained a lucrative position, filed a petition for divorce in order to marry a concubine. There appeared in the courtroom a tired and shabby looking woman, and, on the other hand, her husband, prosperous, self-confident, well-fed and clothed. Similar situations came out in other cases: "we initially had been very happy, when told by my husband that he wanted to become a driver I helped him and maintained the whole family during his training", and then "he joined another woman and... claimed divorce" (D-64); "My husband was studying for the first years of our marriage, and our life was very hard... I was earning and looking after the house as well, because my husband had tuberculosis and needed much care...; after concluding his studies he got a job as assistant lecturer..., met a girl-friend with whom he started to live, and subsequently requested divorce" (D-104) – these are words taken from interviews of divorced women. The trial T-120 took another course: after almost 20 years of undisturbed conjugal life, the husband started drinking, quarrelling, going with other women, beating the wife who was an extremely good wife and mother; eventually he deserted her and two children, leaving them in complete misery, and entered into concubinage. The result was that "there appeared in the court –

according to the motives of the decree issued in this case – an old... broken woman, suffering from heart disease, tuberculous deformation of the backbone and general decrepitude", crooked, depressed, hardly able to walk, with paresis of the right hand. "We begged father to give up his intention of suing" – testified the son of the parties – "because of mother's poor state of health..., father's treatment of mother has been inhuman", and, according to the daughter's evidence given in tears, "after father's departure we were left without any stores for winter, we collected pieces of coal in the streets..., we all asked father to take us with him, but he did not want to... Mother was a wonderful mother and wife... I was educated thanks to my brother's assistance and mother's thrift..., her actual state is the outcome of father's behaviour..., when he had told us about the intended divorce, I begged him to give the idea up as it would be a final blow to mother, I wrote beseeching letters to him, unfortunately without effect". Lastly, in case D-110, described in an interview, the plaintiff deserted his wife, at that time pregnant, and a five-year-old child, during a repatriation journey from Lwów [24] in 1945. He had entered into concubinage, refusing the wife and child the new accommodation which he subsequently acquired. She wandered all over the country, and in the hard post-war conditions could find neither home nor proper job; she bore humiliation and extreme poverty, starved with the child and gave birth to the second child in a railway station, and the husband, informed about the birth of the child, refused to come to her assistance. To maintain the children, she afterwards worked beyond bearing, the more so since the younger child had lung trouble. It was not till some years later that she was advised to sue the husband for alimony, but "the court adjudged a modest reward" because the husband "haggled for every zloty". The children, brought up in hard conditions, were difficult, and the respondent, when interviewed, had coronary thrombosis which was, in her opinion, the result of experiences caused by the marital failure. "I am no longer young" she said, "have neither health nor strength, and am frequently frightened of the insecurity ahead of me; the world seems like a nightmare".

In the light of the data presented here, would the complete rejection of recrimination be morally justified? The answer to the question presumes evaluation, dependant upon the system of ethics held by the one who answers. In the opinion of the present writer it is in the light

[24] A city, until 1939 in Eastern Poland, since the second world war in the Soviet Union.

of just these data that the acceptance of recrimination becomes reasonable: one should not allow the spouse whose conduct has been wicked to such a degree, and who has not considered his liabilities at all, to secure a divorce without any hindrance. It is true that in the situations described here the life together was irreparably broken, and dismissal of the divorce suit would not have inclined the guilty spouse to return to his partner, but if the law enabled him to divorce without any difficulty, it would be equivalent to approval, not condemnation, of his blameworthy behaviour. It would give rise not only to moral repulsion, but also to concern for the impact of law on the human mind, since the law which does not condemn, but approves blameworthy behaviour, demoralies the community instead of educating it.

Thus in the light of the collected data, the reasons for accepting recrimination appear at least as strong as those for its rejection.

5. THE COMPROMISE AND ITS EFFECTS

5.1. Since neither the acceptance nor the rejection of recrimination is fully justified, the legislators were faced with the necessity of finding a compromise which would safeguard the moral values on one hand, and, on the other, also protect the solely guilty spouse in cases in which he deserved protection. The compromise could consist only in acceptance of some limited form of recrimination. The legislators found here a ready pattern in the above mentioned earlier legal systems, and followed it first in Art. 30 of the Family Code of 1950, and afterwards in Art. 56 Para. 3 of the Family and Guardianship Code of 1964. As I have previously said, according to the first of these provisions, divorce could be decreed at the request of the solely guilty spouse only on the condition that his partner consented to divorce or, even in default of consent, if pronouncement of divorce was indicated by the social interest and the spouses had lived apart for a long period; and Art. 56 Para. 3 of the Family and Guardianship Code of 1964 has limited the pronouncement of divorce at request of the solely guilty spouse to those cases in which the innocent partner consents to divorce or the refusal of the consent is contrary to the principles of social co-operation.

What are the practical effects of this compromise? I examined them in the years 1961-1963, i.e. under the rule of Art. 30 of the Family Code, not of Art. 56 Para. 3 of the Family and Guardianship Code; nevertheless, because of close similarity of the two provisions, the collected data throw a clear light upon the working of both. These data, and in particular the figures for dismissals of the divorce trials, indicate that the rule of recrimination leads, at least to some degree, to the achievement of the aim. It appeared that of 153 trials observed a final divorce decree was pronounced in 128, a final dismissal in 11 cases; that is to say that dismissals constituted 7.9 per cent of all the final decrees contained in my sample of trials. In 10 of these 11 cases the exclusive guilt of the plaintiff was the only ground or one of the grounds [25] for dismissal; in other words, 90.9 per cent of dismissals were based on adopting of recrimination. I was unable to find out, for lack of reliable statistical data, whether in all the Polish divorce courts this proportion was equally high. However, according to the information furnished by the judges of Warsaw, Katowice and Lublin, the rule of recrimination is the most common ground for dismissals in their courts as well, and some of them find it to be "the most frequent bar" and "the main restraint" in the divorce suits.

This intended effect is not the only outcome of accepting recrimination. Its acceptance, and in particular its limitation by the innocent spouse's consent to divorce, also results in various additional effects, mostly disadvantageous. The first of them consists in the law's fostering base motives, because of which the innocent spouses frequently refuse to consent. The second is the way in which the consent is obtained: the guilty plaintiffs may pay for consent or use threats to obtain it. Both effects clearly appeared in the course of the present investigations and will be set forth below.

5.2. When refusing to consent to divorce, the innocent spouses are stimulated by various motives. Among them should be mentioned the real desire to preserve the marriage because of lasting affection or because of the children; the desire is frequently connected with the hope of reconciliation. This was the motive which appeared in 11 interviews of the divorcees. Another reason for refusal of consent, met sometimes in interviews as well as in the trials observed, was the innocent spouse's fear of the deterioration of his own financial position: of losing the flat, of losing annuities or social services rendered as a result of the spouse's job, of losing inheritance in the event of the spouse's death. In two trials the defendant gave religious motives for refusal. However, misconduct on the part of the guilty spouse appeared to be the most

[25] Combined with this ground for dismissal were such grounds as incompleteness of breakdown of marriage, or the welfare of the children, contraindicating pronouncement of divorce (cf. p. 23 *et seq.*, *supra*).

frequent reason: here refusal was simply reaction to that behaviour. The examples presented above of a particularly grievous wrong done to the innocent defendant indicate how justifiable this kind of reaction sometimes is; in the light of those examples the words of some of the interrogated women are not surprising: "Why should I have consented? He deserted me after 14 years of married life, I had worked to maintain him, he owes me all he has achieved, and I have neither profession nor anything" (D-86); "he did me too much wrong" (T-80); "I could not forgive him for intending to desert me, an old, invalid woman, as well as the child" (R-9). These words are the more understandable if one takes into account that frequently the solely guilty plaintiffs, because of procedural tactics, not only do not acknowledge their own faults, but also accuse their partners without grounds so as to impute to them the guilt of breakdown: there appears in those cases an additional reason inclining defendants to refuse consent to divorce and to prove their innocence in the further course of the trial. This motive appeared in the courtroom as well as in interviews: "I did not consent to divorce because my husband intended to shift the blame to me" (T-7), "because there were unbelievable lies in the petition" (T-41), "because I did not want to be adjudged on the ground of false charges presented in the petition by my wife" (D-67).

All these reasons seem to be justified; however, the feeling of wrong suffered – a reason of particular import – is separated by a rather vague line from objectionable motives: malice, revengefulness, hatred. Moreover, usually these base motives are connected with the feeling of wrong, and sometimes it is difficult to ascertain whether that feeling or these motives are predominant in inclining the innocent spouse to refuse consent. Thus in the above mentioned case T-134, in which the plaintiff showed symptoms of complete nervous collapse in court, the respondent wife continued with satisfaction her efforts aiming at the dismissal of the petition; and, according to the witnesses' evidence, she had said: "you think, you scoundrel... that I shall give you a divorce? You will die sooner than you will obtain it". In the case T-127 the defendant wife, asked by the court whether decreeing of divorce would be prejudicial to her, answered first: "yes, because I don't want him to live with that woman", and only subsequently added, suggested by her barrister: "I would be satisfied if he returned to me". Several times the women sued, resisting divorce because of malice, justified the resistance on the grounds of affection they alleged to feel for their husbands: "I love him, I am ready to live with him" said one of them in court, and at the same time she accused him with evident hatred (T-81). Similar reasons came out in some interviews of divorced persons: "my husband did it to spite me, he wanted to make my life more difficult" and therefore did not consent to divorce (D-83). I did not consent "in order to find some satisfaction, the only requital accessible was not to assist him... The court should never give such an old scoundrel a divorce... That there was a child? What does it matter, that minx should suffer" (D-38). These observations were confirmed by the experience of judges and barristers. I asked all the 41 judges and 60 barristers interviewed, "for what reasons do the innocent defendants refuse to consent to divorce?". Since almost every subject interviewed mentioned several motives, I asked them to range the motives in order of frequency and intensity. Among them were: the desire to preserve the marriage because of affection or because of children, various financial reasons, religious beliefs, a feeling of wrong suffered, fear of the opinion of their acquaintances; however, none of these motives was mentioned so frequently as hatred, revenge and wish to spite the plaintiff: these base motives were mentioned by 39 judges and 59 barristers. Of these 14 (i.e. 34.1 per cent) of the judges, and 35 (i.e. 58.3 per cent) of the barristers held them to be the most frequent and intense; the difference between the proportion of judges and barristers of this opinion can easily be explained: the parties are more disposed to make their discreditable motives known frankly in the barrister's office than in the courtroom.

Thus the rule of recrimination, limited by the innocent spouse's consent, acts in favour of those whose motives do not deserve approval. The collected data indicate how prevalent this was under the rule of Art. 30 of the Family Code of 1950. The situation resulted in some counteraction on the part of the divorce courts: seeing the defendant refuse to consent to divorce from base motives, the court sometimes tended to disregard the rule of recrimination, in particular in cases in which the plaintiff, in the light of the collected evidence, deserved assistance despite his fault. This tendency had appeared in some earlier decisions of the Supreme Court; it also came out in the trials observed by myself: the court either persuaded the innocent spouse to consent to divorce, or attempted to construct the common guilt of both parties.

These expedients were, however, inadequate, because of the scope of the phenomenon which I am talking about. Thence – the tendency toward changing the law. This tendency resulted first in some previous draft codes, and eventually in Art. 56 Para. 3 of the present Family and

Guardianship Code, enabling the court to pronounce divorce even against the innocent defendant's will, if the refusal is "contrary to the principles of social co-operation".

Art. 56 Para. 3 was enforced in 1965, and it is too early to judge what its results will be, and in particular whether it will effectively counteract reprehensible action on the part of the innocent defendants; nevertheless, the data collected under the rule of art. 30 of the Family Code enable a safe guess on this point.

These data justify the hope that the new provision would not be applied in too liberal a manner. The contents of Art. 56 Para. 3 may, indeed, cause some anxiety: a judge who in general is against recrimination would possibly be inclined to consider almost every refusal of consent as contrary to the rules of social co-operation, which would in practice mean the cancelling of recrimination. This anxiety does not, however, seem justifiable. I asked, when the Family Code of 1950 was still in force, all the 41 judges interviewed to give their opinion on the divorce provisions in force and to make proposals *de lege ferenda:* 36 of them held those provisions to be right or proposed some amendments unconnected with recrimination. The remaining 5 of them suggested the introduction of changes concerning recrimination: one of them proposed its sharpening, four – its limiting, but only in the cases in which refusal of consent to divorce appeared as harassment; and no judge declared for any further limiting of recrimination. Consequently, since the judges are not against recrimination, Art. 56 Para. 3 will probably not be interpreted in too liberal a manner.

Another matter is whether, and to what degree, the new rule would correct the practice existing up to this time, supporting those who refuse consent from base motives. The collected data indicate that no marked improvement can be expected. Even under Art. 30 of the Family Code some of the innocent defendants hid the reprehensible motives of refusal from the court even though making them known would not, in principle, influence the court's decision. This concealment became evident in interviewing those divorced women who, according to the court's records, had given affection as the reason for refusal of consent, and in the interview openly displayed malice and revengefulness as the real motives: "the only requital accessible was not to assist him" (D-38), "I wanted to keep him waiting, let him suffer since he is so clever" (D-118). The attempt to conceal base motives also appeared in the courtroom, in cases in which it was unsuccessful[26]. Moreover, their concealment was

[26] These were, in particular, the cases T-127 and T-81 quoted on pp. 127-128, *supra.*

indicated by the above mentioned difference between the experiences of judges and barristers: only 34.1 per cent of judges and as many as 58.3 per cent of barristers found those motives the strongest and most common, which, as I previously explained, was due to the fact that the parties are rather disinclined to reveal their own discreditable attitudes in the courtroom. It is clear that they will hide them even more under the rule of Art. 56 Para. 3 of the Family and Guardianship Code, since, according to the new provision, it has become certain that revealing them would make the defendant's opposition to divorce ineffective: therefore the defendants who refuse to consent for such reasons will even more frequently feign affection and concern for children. It is true that concealment will not always be effective: where emotions prevail over reasons of procedural tactics, the real motives do come out in court; and they come out if other manifest activities of the innocent defendant – e.g. incriminations brought against the spouse to the public prosecutor – indicate revengefulness and hatred. In these evident cases the new rule will apparently result in some improvement. It is, however, almost certain that evident cases will seldom occur: malice, revenge, hatred will probably be hidden in most cases, and those who are able to hide them – the least scrupulous and the slyest – will succeed under the rule of the new provision as well.

5.3. Another additional effect of accepting of recrimination limited by the innocent spouse's consent is abusing of recrimination in order to achieve financial gains: according to speculations shortly after the enactment of the previous Family Code of 1950, the limiting of recrimination by consent "gives the spouses an opportunity for machinations" which consists mainly in the "buying of consent for money"; moreover, "sometimes the innocent spouse exploits his guilty partner and demands a high price for divorce" [27].

The present investigations indicate that there are frequently cases of various forms of reward offered for consent to divorce. It was made known first in interviews of the 131 divorcees who described their own divorce trials. In 30 of those trials the defendant consented to divorce in spite of the fact that the plaintiff's guilt was – according to the court's records and contents of the interview – either exclusive or predominant to a degree which justified his being charged with exclusive guilt and dismissing the suit in default of his partner's consent.

[27] J. Gwiazdomorski, M. Grudzinski, S. Kaleta, A. Wolter, *op. cit.*, pp. 66, 67.

I put additional questions to all the subjects interviewed who had been divorced as result of those 30 trials. The additional questions varied. For instance, if they were addressed to an innocent woman sued by her guilty partner, I asked her first: "Why did you consent to divorce?", and afterwards: "How did your husband reward your consent?". If they were addressed to a solely guilty plaintiff, the first of them was: "Why did your wife consent to divorce", the second: "what did she demand of you for giving her consent?, the third: "how did you reward her consent?". According to the answers obtained, in 11 of those 30 trials – i.e. in 36.7 per cent – the defendant's consent was rewarded: this proportion makes clear the scope of the phenomenon under discussion. It was difficult to ascertain whether this proportion is equally high all over the country. Nevertheless, the barristers' information indicated that, on a wider scale as well, the figure for paid consents is considerable. Only 17 of the 60 barristers interviewed declared that they had never had to do with a payment; it is not possible to exclude the likelihood that some of them gave false answers in order to avoid mentioning rewards with an illegal flavour in the trials they had themselves conducted. The 43 remaining barristers had experience of payments in their practice: they had had to do with them altogether in approximately 324 cases which means 7.6 per cent of all the divorce trials conducted by all the barristers interviewed. I could not, however, find out what proportion of all the consents to divorce, given guilty spouses by their innocent partners, was represented by those 324 payments: the majority of the barristers were unable to ascertain how many of such consents they had known in their practice.

The property given in payment for consent to divorce differs. The divorcees and barristers mentioned here various kinds of assets: higher alimony, vacating of the common flat, unequal division of the matrimonial property [28], transfer of movables or of real property, the giving of a sum of money which, in the barristers' reports, varied from 2 to 200 thousand zlotys, the most frequent values amounting to 5, 10, 20, 50 and 100 thousand [29].

The very form of these rewards suggests that not all of them deserve to be evaluated in a similar way. Some of them are payments *sensu stricto* and are making a business of divorce; in the words of one of

[28] In which, according to provisions of the Polish Family and Guardianship Code, both spouses have, in principle, equal shares after divorce.

[29] The average monthly remuneration of working people in Poland being around 2000 zlotys (as I mentioned above, p. 59, footnote 38).

the judges interviewed "there are women who know particularly well how to sell their marriage" (J-3). "My barrister convinced me that it would be nonsense to disagree to divorce, because my husband would never return anyway, and advised that I should get as much money as possible", said one of the women interviewed; "I therefore wanted to obtain the highest price possible..., that was the only moment when my husband was ready, in order to arrange his affairs, to give any sum; he declared he would make an alimony allowance amounting to 1500 zlotys per month, and gave, in addition, 120 thousand" (D-104). Another woman interviewed said: "I consented to divorce for the money, it was simply a sale of divorce" (D-107). She intended, moreover, to cheat her husband: "I wanted to promise him my consent in order to incline him to payment, and afterwards not to consent: to take the money and not give a divorce; but he is clever: not till I consented to divorce did he give me the money". Abuses of this kind frequently occur, and the barristers and judges interviewed gave several instances: "the plaintiff had given his defendant wife various valuable objects..., she had taken them for the promise of consent, but subsequently refused to consent and the trial finally resulted in dismissal" (B-38); the plaintiff "had paid his wife 100 thousand zlotys for consent to divorce, she had accepted the money, and then refused to consent; the refusal was followed by another trial for recovery of the money paid", and the judge who furnished the information had conducted the trial (J-25); and another judge was in charge of a trial for 10 thousand "which the husband had in writing promised his wife for consent" and did not pay in spite of her consenting (J-9).

It is clear that this kind of payment merits disapproval: making a business of divorce is objectionable, and not only in cases in which it is combined with the desire to cheat the partner. Nevertheless, such transactions are frequently just within a step of reward which seems justifiable, that is of damages for wrong done the innocent spouse by the breakdown of marriage.

The damage caused the innocent partner may be pecuniary or immaterial. Various kinds of pecuniary losses appeared in the trials observed and in the interviews. Among them were losses caused by drunkards selling the contents of the common home in order to get money for alcohol, loss of accommodation, loss of earning abilities as result of deterioration of health caused by marital failure and costs of medical care, expenses connected with the divorce suit, loss of economic status which the marriage gave the innocent spouse, usually the wife. This last is particularly acute in the above described situation in which the wife, sacrificing herself to the interests of her husband and home, did not acquire any professional training, and, because of age, state of health or duties to children, has become unable to acquire it in the future. The alimony allowances due after divorce are usually an insufficient compensation: the liable spouse frequently evades his duty, hides his income from the court, sometimes charges himself, after divorce, with new liabilities which limit his duty to pay alimony to the wife and child of the divorced wedlock. Hence the frequent complaints of divorced women about the amount of alimony awarded by the court and about evading of payment: "the husband has a free hand... and all my earnings go to provide for the children's needs", because the court "ordered him to pay only a modest allowance...: the court did not take into account that something is due to me..., I am in extreme financial difficulties..., why does the law never gain an insight into the living conditions of mother and children after divorce?" (D-110); "I am bringing up three children on 1000 zlotys per month, because my husband does not pay anything" (D-54); the husband "has acquaintances among court executive officers and gets out of his duties" (D-53); the husband "was sentenced to two years' imprisonment for malicious failure to pay alimony", and in spite of that "he still does not pay" (D-62).

Despite the hardship caused by all those pecuniary losses, the incorporeal harm seems to be even greater: this is the pain caused by breakdown of marriage and divorce. The present investigations indicate how intense it is. I have spoken above of the intensity of suffering resulting from marital failure, preceding pronouncement of divorce. The suffering appearing after divorce has been reported in the interviews of persons divorced, in particular of women. They suffered a harassing feeling of loneliness and longed for the husband's return: "I am sure he will come back to me again..., I will take him back" (D-38); "I am ready to be reconciled any time" (D-86); I married again, because "I couldn't remain alone, I must have somebody to live for, but I never concealed from my present husband that I don't know whether I shall ever forget the man who was my greatest and only love" (D-45). The women interviewed also told of their unsuccessful search for a new partner, and some of them spoke of obsessive fear of the former husband's return and aversion to marriage in general: "I am disgusted with men, I shall never marry again" (D-122); "Life is so quiet now, I am afraid all the time my husband will suddenly come back", my life with him "was so horrifying" that I still cannot "shake it off and calm myself" (D-26). The sufferings of divorcees are increased by difficulties in the upbringing of children in the broken family: "I had to leave the four-year-old boy alone the whole day. I taught him to heat up the meals..., I was in extreme difficulties..., the court awarded 100 zlotys per month for the child's maintenance" (D-26); "I worked from 7 a.m. till 10 p.m., the children were uncared for, the older son neglected study and failed at school..., the younger is at a very difficult period, he is repeating his class at school..., is in trouble with police..., I can't help it, and have no assistance or understanding from anyone" (D-110). Failures of health which divorced women connected with breakdown of marriage, in particular heart and nervous diseases, were reported again and again, as well as the feeling of wrong suffered and helplessness. There continually came out a vivid and emotional reaction to the problem of divorce which appeared, "for the majority of subjects interviewed, the most vital issue" [30]. The following are two instances of remarks summing up each interview and concerning its course: "the respondent's nerves were so much on an edge that she was crying most of the time..., divorce is to the present day a disaster for her" (D-92). "I would rather not have had to talk about it, this is a very painful matter" – complained another woman divorced –; "when this letter of yours reached me I became so upset by the renewal of the affair that I could not sleep. After the present talk I shall be ill again, I can neither speak nor think quietly about all that" (D-98).

All the above mentioned facts are just examples: I had no intention of measuring the losses caused by breakdown of marriage and divorce; and in particular, I did not intend to measure the suffering arising from divorce [31]. Nevertheless, the collected examples indicate how grievous these injuries are, the pecuniary as well as incorporeal. The duty of compensating the harm sustained in consequence of an injury has become a common characteristic of contemporary legislations. The injuries which I am talking about also gave rise, in Poland, to the duty of making compensation: according to Art. 29 of the Law of Marriage of 1945, "in the decree pronouncing divorce the court shall, at request of the innocent spouse, award him, from the guilty partner, damages

[30] Words of the interviewer, Mrs. T. Dobrowolska, contained in her general remarks on the interviews obtained.

[31] The divorce trauma was measured in an admirable study by W. J. Goode, *After Divorce* (Glencoe, Illinois, 1956), p. 185 *et seq.*, who applied to the measurement the Lazarsfeld technique.

for harm caused by divorce and by behaviour which resulted in divorce; moreover, the court may award him damages for anguish". This provision, which had been in accord with a widely accepted feeling of justice, was set aside in 1950; it is not to be found in the Family Code of 1950 or in the present Family and Guardianship Code of 1964. The setting aside of the first part of it which established damages for pecuniary losses, was caused by the fact that the innocent spouse could also get damages for them on the ground of norms contained in the law of torts [32]. On the other hand, the rejecting of its further part was due to a more general tendency: the negative attitude of socialist law toward damages for anguish.

It is an old tendency, based upon an idea which has always been advocated, but about 1950 gained in strength in Poland: the idea of the immorality of giving money in compensation for sufferings. In the foregoing period there were a number of provisions establishing damages for anguish. There was among them, in particular, Art. 165 of the former Code of Obligations of 1934 which enforced damages for anguish "in the case of bodily injury or derangement of health, deprivation of... freedom, insult", and in the case in which "either a woman, or a man under age or mentally handicapped was, by means of deceit, violence, abuse of dependency or taking advantage of a critical situation, induced to submit to an indecent act". According to Art. 166 of the Code of Obligations, "if the bodily injury or derangement of health resulted in death", the court could allow "the person nearest to the deceased or an institution indicated by them a suitable sum of money as damages for anguish". Also the former family law, in force till 1950, allowed damages for anguish due to the mother of an illegitimate child if marriage had been promised to her. Provisions based upon a similar idea were also contained in the other branches of the law, e.g. in the Law of Copyright.

All these provisions were, however, sharply criticised in the fifties. "The compensating of moral suffering with money" was regarded as an idea "born on the ground of capitalist conditions, alien to socialist law" [33], characteristic of "the bourgeois approach to the problem of protecting personal rights" [34]. In the opinion of the critics, this idea

[32] In Poland the norms of the law of torts constitute one of the branches of the Civil Code.

[33] S. Szer, "Kodeks rodzinny" ("The Family Code") in *Demokratyczny Przeglad Prawniczy* (1950/3). p. 8.

[34] A. Wolter, *Prawo cywilne - czesc ogólna (General Part of the Civil Law)* (Warsaw, 1955), p. 153.

could have arisen "only on the foundations of a fetishism of money" and indicates a decline in the moral qualities of its followers, since "the rating of human suffering in terms of money and its compensating with money" is contradictory to "the elementary moral values and human dignity" [35]. As a consequence of this criticism the idea of complete setting aside of damages for anguish was advocated.

However, not all the opinions expessed in the fifties were against damages for anguish. Those for damages put forward several arguments. Firstly – its compensative value in enabling the injured party to obtain various facilities and comforts which can, at least to some degree, relieve his pain [36]. Moreover, they indicated its particular compensative value in cases in which the pecuniary loss cannot be easily measured or is not palpable: damages for anguish can then become the proper compensation [37]. They also pointed out the preventive and repressive role which damages for anguish play, besides sanctions known to criminal law [38]. All these arguments justify, in their opinion, the maintaining of damages for anguish in socialist law.

Because of the divergent views the legislators, following several constructive decisions of the Supreme Court, finally accepted a compromise solution. It retained, in Art. 445 of the present Civil Code [39], damages for anguish in the case of bodily injury or derangement of health, of deprivation of freedom, and of causing a woman, "by means of deceit, violence or abuse of dependency, to submit to an indecent act". On the other hand, it set aside many other provisions establishing damages for anguish. Thus the present Civil Code does not allow damages for suffering connected with the death of the nearest person, damages for anguish are unknown in the Law of Copyright, and – an important issue from the point of view of the present considerations – they are unknown in family law, in particular they are not due for the suffering caused by breakdown of marriage and divorce.

35 M. Wawiłowa, "Zadoscuczynienie za krzywde moralna w prawie polskim" (Damages for Anguish in the Polish Law") in *Nowe Prawo* (1954/6), pp. 1020/1021.

36 A. Kedzierska, "W sprawie zadoscuczynienia za krzywde moralna" ("On the Problem of Damages for Anguish") in *Panstwo i Prawo* (1955/I), pp. 270, 271; A. Szpunar, "Czyny niedozwolone w projekcie kodeksu cywilnego" ("The Law of Torts in the Draft of the Civil Code") in *Nowe Prawo* (1955/2), pp. 24-26; Z. Radwanski, *Zadoscuczynienie pieniezne za szkode niemajatkowa (The Damages for Incorporeal Injury)* (Poznan, 1956), p. 142 *et seq.*

37 A. Kedzierska, *ibid;* S. Grzybowski, *Prawo wynalazcze (The Law of Inventions)* (Warsaw, 1956), p. 186.

38 A. Kedzierska, *op. cit.*, p. 271-273; Z. Radwanski, *op. cit.*, pp. 153, 154.

39 In force since January 1, 1965.

The present paper does not aim at resolving the above-described controversy, or at evaluating the legislative compromise in which the controversy resulted. For the use of these considerations it is enough to ascertain that damages for anguish caused by divorce have been set aside in Polish law. The collected factual data throw light on some effects of its setting aside. Namely, it emerged that, on the part of divorcees, there appeared an intense need for broad compensation embracing damages for anguish. I did not ask the subjects interviewed about this need: it was spontaneously disclosed by them, in particular by eight from among those divorced women whose husbands were solely or chiefly guilty of the breakdown. "He gave me nothing, not any compensation" – complained one of them – "I hoped the court would compel him to pay something" (D-72). The second one was promised by the husband that he would give her "some money, he gave it, but it was a small sum in relation to the wrong suffered" (D-125). And one of them, sued by a faithless drunkard and rowdy who neglected her and the child and did not contribute to the maintenance of the family, had requested in the court that "he should give at least something for all that"; she got nothing and no longer trusts "any courts, any authorities", now she knows "how much indifference to human suffering and to truth there is" (D-53). In the above mentioned case D-110 the woman interviewed had a similar grudge against the court: "the court did not take into account that something is due to me for my youth so hopelessly worn away..., I didn't get a penny; he... had not been concerned for 14 years with my helplessness and the children's..., and the court gave him a divorce finding him guilty: I suppose some compensation should have been given me...; it was due to him that my life was ruined; the law helped him in this".

These claims and complaints on the part of divorced women are understandable in the light of the above described wrongs suffered. They are the more understandable if one takes into account that the usual way of claiming damages on the ground of the law of torts is – despite the above mentioned opinion of those who are against damages for divorce – insufficient. For, if the damage consists, as in the last instance, in the "youth worn away", if it consists in the loss of strength and general deterioration of health, not being a definite disease, or in the losing of chances in life and the ability of social adaptation – no court will award damages for those losses on the ground of the law of torts, despite their painfulness: they can hardly be measured and are not definite enough to be compensated in the usual trial for damages.

On the other hand it is possible – and this has been indicated, in another connection, by the Supreme Court – to claim them in the form of damages for anguish. This possibility was felt not only by the women injured. It was also pointed out by some of the judges and barristers who were for the introducing of damages for pecuniary and incorporeal harm caused by marital failure and divorce, in order to endow the injured and weaker partner "with an equal start with the guilty spouse" (J-3).

It seems that in the light of those data the compensative function of reward paid by the guilty spouse for his innocent partner's consent to divorce emerges clearly. The legislators set aside the broad treatment of damages for breakdown of marriage and divorce in order to limit it to the damages established by the law of torts. The needs of those who come to the divorce court are for the broad treatment. These needs appear to be stronger than restrictive provisions: they are met in the form of payments for the innocent spouse's consent. The fact that a considerable number of divorcees regard the payments in this way has been emphasised by themselves in interviews. It is even more interesting that the behaviour of judges indicates the same point of view: some of them do initiate this form of damages. This initiative appeared three times in the course of my investigations, including twice in the courtroom. "There is no harm in the husband paying; there is a gap in the Family Code" said the judge to the parties in the case T-49. "You should get damages", he said to the wife, "you have educated the child". Then he turned to the husband: "you are guilty..., you earn 4000 and your wife 1300", and subsequently to both parties: "Please, do agree to the amount, it is better to do so in the court than outside". The parties agreed to the sum due and the agreement was recorded under the form of a would-be alimony arrear. In the case T-153 another judge explicitly persuaded the solely guilty plaintiff to pay damages in order to incline his partner to consent to divorce. And one of the barristers, in an interview which I ranked among those most deserving confidence, told of the particularly far-reaching initiative of one of the judges: the judge "took, in the courtroom, 12,000 zlotys from the husband's hand and delivered them to the wife, saying: since it is due, you must pay; if you don't pay, divorce won't be decreed" (B-31).

How should one evaluate, in the light of the collected data, the paying for the innocent spouse's consent? It seems that it does not merit a clear evaluation. Some of the payments certainly deserve disapproval: they are those which make a business of divorce. The others are requested as a compensation for damage and are so much in accord with the broadly accepted feeling of justice that even judges initiate them. Nevertheless, in the legislators' opinion all of them should be condemned. As I mentioned above, Art. 30 of the Family Code, under the rule of which the present investigations have been carried out, was substituted by Art. 56 Para. 3 of the Family and Guardianship Code. Art. 56 Para. 3 makes pronouncement of divorce claimed by the solely guilty spouse dependent upon the consent of the innocent, unless the refusal of this consent is contrary to the principles of social co-operation. This change was introduced in order to make ineffective the refusal of consent caused by base motives: malice, hatred, revengefulness. It was, however, not the only purpose of the change: according to the opinion expressed by the Commission of Administration of Justice of the Seym [40], the introduction of the new provision was also justified by the fact that cases occur of "making consent to divorce dependent on payment of reward" [41]. Thus the legislators not only disapproved of all the kinds of reward for divorce, but made refusal of consent caused by the wish for a reward equivalent to refusal caused by the above mentioned base motives. The new provision has been introduced in order to prevent the claiming of payments. It is too early to ascertain the effectiveness of the change, but the present investigations again justify a safe guess: it will probably not be effective. There are two ways in which Art. 56 Para. 3 could effectively prevent payment for consent. First – if it resulted in pronouncement of divorce without the innocent spouse's consent in cases in which consent was refused in order to get a reward. In those cases, however, pronouncement of divorce would be conditioned upon the presentation of evidence that refusal of consent was caused by the desire to gain payment; and this evidence can hardly ever be given, since the payment is not usually demanded either in a written document or in presence of witnesses, the more so if the law disapproves the demand. Another way in which the new provision could prevent paying for consent would be its liberal interpretation by the courts, recognizing almost every refusal of consent as contrary to the rules of social co-operation, which would in practice mean the cancelling of recrimination; the acceptance of this interpretation by the courts would cause, among those who come to the divorce court, the feeling that the court would pronounce divorce irrespective of the plaintiff's

[40] The Polish Parliament.
[41] Poprawki do kodeksu rodzinnego i opiekunczego (Amendments to the Family and Guardianship Code) in *Trybuna Ludu* of February 10, 1964.

unilateral guilt: such an impression would restrain the solely guilty spouses from paying for consent. However, as I have said above, in the light of the judges' views, the accepting of the liberal interpretation is not likely. Consequently, it seems that the new provision will neither liquidate nor clearly limit payments for consent.

5.4. The last of the additional effects of recrimination limited by the innocent spouse's consent is the obtaining of consent without or even against his will. It was conjectured shortly after the enactment of the Family Code of 1950, that consent was sometimes obtained "by means of... pressure" [42]. This conjecture is correct; cases of pressure do occur, and they came out in the course of the present investigations: there was either compulsion to consent to divorce because of the plaintiff's guilt or, more frequently, to divorce without deciding the question of guilt.

In the courtroom such pressure came out only twice. "My husband threatened me that if I didn't agree to divorce... he would destroy all things that I had at home" said the wife in the case T-93, "I don't agree to divorce because of this blackmail, but because we could never live together any more"; "I agree to divorce", said another one, "because my husband said, when I visited him in prison, that he would kill me if I disagree" (T-132). In the first of these cases the wife was not afraid of the threats, in the second – the threatening husband was absent, and probably that was why the pressure came out. However, for the most part the pressure does not come out in the courtroom; if it is effective, the party under constraint hides it from the court. In consequence, the judges asked about the number of threats met with in their practice usually answered they had never come across them or were unable to estimate their number. They had never been met by 24 out of 41 judges interviewed. 7 others expressed only suppositions: "I suppose it happens" (J-31), "I think it happened twice or three times, but I am not certain" (J-34). A further 9 judges had met attempts to force consent made known by the parties in the court. They were, obviously, ineffective attempts, since the court, when it realized the pressure, dismissed the petition: "if we see pressure we don't give a divorce" (J-29); the husband forced the wife's consent "in five of the suits tried by me, but... he did not obtain divorce" (J-2). Only one judge confessed he had granted divorce despite pressure: he was told about the compulsion by a third person, "but after divorce had been pronounced" (J-1).

[42] J. Gwiazdomorski, M. Grudzinski, S. Kaleta, A. Wolter, *op. cit.*, p. 67.

In contradistinction to the parties who had hidden the coercion from the court, the divorcees interviewed recited it without fear and more frankly. I have said above that in 30 of the suits described by 131 divorcees the defendant consented to divorce in spite of the fact that the plaintiff's guilt was either exclusive or predominant. Here again, in order to find out the pressures, I put additional questions to all the subjects interviewed who had been divorced as a result of those 30 trials. These questions varied. For instance, if they were addressed to an innocent woman sued by her guilty partner, I asked her first: "Why did you consent to divorce?", and afterwards: "Did your husband compel you to consent, and if so, how?". If they were addressed to a solely guilty plaintiff whose wife had refused to consent in the initial part of the suit, but then agreed to divorce, the first question was: "Why did your wife not consent to divorce at the beginning of the suit?", the second: "Did you attempt to compel her to consent, and if so, how?", the third: "Why did your wife consent to divorce in the course of the suit?". According to the answers obtained, in 4 of these 30 trials – i.e. in 13.3 per cent – the pressure of the plaintiff was the only reason or one of the reasons for consent. It is quite possible that the real proportion was even higher; for, one cannot be certain whether all the subjects who had compelled their partners to consent confessed it in the interviews.

I intended to find out whether in the other courts under my investigations the forcing of consent is involved in divorce so frequently; however, the question could not be answered. Here the judges' information was of no value, because of the threats being hidden from them. It seemed that the barristers might furnish more reliable data. It appeared, however, that their information was far from being as accurate as that concerning payments for consent: they said in the interviews that threats, in contradistinction to payments for consent, "do not come out despite the fact that they occur rather frequently" (B-16), and are not revealed "in the courtroom nor even in the barrister's office" (B-13). This is possibly due to the fact that the parties, when aiming at obtaining payment for consent, frequently turn to the barristers for advice or even mediation, while in the event of threats his assistance may only sometimes be of use to the endangered spouse. Hence, only 17 of the 60 barristers interviewed said that they had met effective pressure which resulted in divorce; the others had only met with attempts to force consent. Those who had come across effective pressure were asked how frequently. They mentioned altogether approximately 41 cases. It seems that this figure is much lower than the real number, unknown to the barristers, of effective enforcements which occurred in the 4,280 divorce trials conducted by them.

On the other hand, the data collected in the court and in interviews of barristers clearly indicate what kind of pressure is most frequent. As I have said, there appeared in the courtroom threats of murder and demolishing of the matrimonial home. The other threats came out in the interviews of the above mentioned 4 divorced persons. There were among them 3 defendant women and a plaintiff husband who confessed that he had compelled his wife to consent. The plaintiff threatened he would report the wife's criminal offence to the authorities; the defendants made known other kinds of pressure: "he maltreated, kicked and beat me, and constantly shouted: 'Give me a divorce; if you don't, I'll show you!' " (D-118); "he said that if I don't consent to divorce, he would not give any money..., when I refused to consent at the first sitting, he ceased to pay" (D-127); "he threatened that he would throw me out of the dwelling..., that he would not pay for the child's maintenance..., I was afraid I would become completely worn out, I had to give up" (D-43). There were also the barristers interviewed who had met threats of physical force, of committing suicide, reporting the defendant's criminal offence to the authorities, discontinuing payment of alimony, etc.

The compelling of consent warrants disapproval: it restrains the effectiveness of recrimination and the restraint eventuates in favour of the least scrupulous. Such intimidation seems, however, to be an unavoidable consequence of the legislative compromise which consists in making divorce at request of the solely guilty spouse dependent on his partner's consent. For, the court does not have any instrument enabling it to ascertain whether the consent is freely given. No such instrument existed under the previous Family Code, nor does it exist under the rule of the current divorce provisions.

5.5. Thus the most important effects – both intended and accidental ones – of the compromise adopted by the Polish divorce law have been discussed above. Consequently, there may arise the question of how the compromise deserves to be evaluated. Yet, may I be permitted to leave that question unanswered, for two reasons. First, my intention was rather to learn about and discuss recrimination as a working institution than to express my personal views. Secondly, any clear evaluation would here be extremely difficult. The Polish legislators did not reject recrimination, for moral and educative reasons, nor enforce it without limits, in order to avoid treating the solely guilty spouse too harshly. It seems, in the light of the collected data, that the rule of recrimination does not establish the motivation of behaviour aimed at; on the other hand, it undoubtedly meets an important moral demand, though the demand has been treated here in a manner which differs from that of the legislators. Meeting this demand, the rule of recrimination results, mainly because of its limiting by the innocent spouse's consent, in various unintended effects, sometimes contrary to the legislators' views. For these reasons it would be difficult to evaluate unambiguously the working of the norms under discussion; like any other compromise, it can only result in partially achieving the intended goals. However, the problem which I have been discussing is so complex, and remains so much under the strong influence of divergent tendencies, that the avoidance of a compromise in its solution would not seem practical.

CONCLUSION

These considerations are of a monographic character: they are based mainly on an examination of a part of the practice of the Cracow Court and of some fragments of the practice of three other divorce courts; this means a modest empirical basis. These considerations justify therefore qualitative rather than quantitative generalizations, and only with this provision may be regarded, by a comparative lawyer or sociologist, as a report on the law in action in an East European country. It is, however, possible that the present investigations will be continued. If this is the case, and if the samples drawn are broader, a transition to quantitative generalizations will become practical. It will not only mean an achievement of a higher level of knowledge, but it may also contribute better to the comparative science of living law, and, moreover, supply in the long run a firmer basis for future legislations.

BLANKS OF SOME OF THE QUESTIONNAIRES USED

Questionnaire for divorced persons (wives[1]) belonging to the sample D-1 – 131

(in yes-and-no questions the appropriate point should be underlined)

1. a.[2] During the whole divorce trial there was agreement between you and your husband:
    as to divorce without deciding the question of guilt[3]
    as to divorce because of your guilt[3]
    as to divorce because of your husband's guilt[3]
    Did that agreement appear:
        before filing the petition?
        after filing the petition?
   b.[2] In the course of the divorce trial there came an agreement between you and your husband:
    as to divorce without deciding the question of guilt[3]
    as to divorce because of your guilt[3]
    as to divorce because of your husband's guilt[3]
    Was the agreement an outcome of:
    the advice of the barrister (or barristers of both parties)?
    the advice of the judge?
    someone else's advice, and if so, whose (what was his relation to the parties)?
    ....

[1] An analogous questionnaire was directed to husbands.

[2] Questions a. and b. were asked alternatively. On the basis of court records, before handing the questionnaire to the interviewer, I chose one of those questions; or I eliminated both if the contest did not die out until conclusion of the suit.

[3] Before handing the questionnaire to the interviewer I underlined, on the basis of court records, one of the points here mentioned.

you and your husband reaching the conclusion that the case should be settled without contest?
(In the case of more than one affirmative answer to the above questions, all the points chosen should be underlined, and, moreover, the one which, in the respondent's opinion, most influenced reaching an agreement, should be marked with a cross).

2. Do you remember the conciliatory session (i.e. the first sitting of the court, at which the judge tried to bring you to reconciliation)?
yes no
(if yes) Did the conciliatory session check your will to obtain a divorce?
yes no no answer
In your opinion, did the conciliatory session check your husband's will to obtain a divorce?
yes no don't know
How did the judge try to bring you to reconciliation?
....

3. Did the divorce suit as such make relations between you and your partner more bitter than they had been before it began?
yes no no answer
(if yes) Why?
....
In your opinion, was there a chance of reconciliation before bringing the suit?
yes no no answer

4. a.[4] (Questions addressed to an innocent wife who, being sued by her guilty partner, consented to divorce)
Why did you consent to divorce?
....
How did your husband reward your consent?
....

[4] Questions a., b., c., d., e. and f. were asked alternatively. On the basis of court records, before handing the questionnaire to the interviewer, I chose one of those questions. Sometimes, however, the choice made had to be changed in the course of the interview, under the influence of information furnished by the respondent.

Did your husband compel you to consent, and if so, how?

....

b.[5] (Questions addressed to an innocent wife who, being sued by her guilty partner, did not consent to divorce)

Why did you not consent to divorce?

....

What did you demand of your husband for giving consent?

....

Did he attempt to compel you to consent, and if so, how?

....

c.[5] Questions addressed to an innocent wife who, being sued by her guilty partner, had refused to consent in the initial part of the suit, but then agreed to divorce)

Why did you not consent to divorce at the beginning of the suit?

....

What did you demand of your husband for giving consent?

....

Did your husband attempt to compel you to consent, and if so, how?

....

Why did you consent in the course of the suit?

....

How did your husband reward your consent?

....

d.[5] (Questions addressed to a solely guilty plaintiff wife whose husband consented to divorce)

Why did your husband consent to divorce?

....

What did he demand of you for giving his consent?

....

How did you reward his consent?

....

e.[5] (Questions addressed to a solely guilty plaintiff wife whose husband did not consent to divorce)

Why did your husband not consent to divorce?

....

What did he demand of you for giving his consent?

....

[5] See p. 146, footnote 4.

Did you attempt to induce him to consent, and if so, how?

....

f.[6] (Questions addressed to a solely guilty plaintiff wife whose husband had refused to consent in the initial part of the suit, but then consented to divorce)

Why did your husband not consent to divorce at the beginning of the suit?

....

What did he demand of you for giving his consent?

....

Did you attempt to induce him to consent, and if so, how?

....

Why did he consent to divorce in the course of the suit?

....

How did you reward his consent?

....

5. Was your barrister informed about the state of your marriage, and in particular about conflicts between you and your spouse:
   very accurately?
   rather accurately?
   knew only some circumstances?
   knew nothing or almost nothing?

6. What do you think now: if the court had dismissed the petition for divorce, would you have become reconciled?
   probably become reconciled?
   probably not become reconciled?
   certainly not become reconciled?
   don't know

7. Do you think that, in your husband's opinion, you would have become reconciled?
   probably become reconciled?
   probably not become reconciled?
   certainly not become reconciled?
   don't know

[6] See p. 146, footnote 4.

8. Have you any further comments on the divorce suit or other problems which we have been talking about?

   ....

9. Remarks on the respondent

   ....

10. Remarks on the course of the interview

   ....

Questionnaire for reconciled persons

1. Do you remember the conciliatory session (i.e. the first sitting in the court, at which the judge tried to bring you to reconciliation)?

   yes no

   (if yes) Did the conciliatory session check your will to obtain a divorce?

   yes no no answer

   In your opinion, did the conciliatory session check your husband's (wife's) will to obtain a divorce?

   yes no don't know

   How did the judge try to bring you to reconciliation?

   ....

2. Did you become reconciled due to:

   1°– persuasion of the judge at the conciliatory session?

   2°– persuasion of the judge in the further course of the trial?

   3°– what other circumstances?

   ....

3. Do you think that you will never stand before the divorce court again?

   ....

4. Does your husband (wife) share this view?

   ....

5. Don't you regret reconciliation?

   ....

6. In your opinion, does your husband (wife) regret reconciliation?

   ....

7. Have you any further comments on the divorce suit or other problems which we have been talking about?

   ....

8. Remarks on the respondent

   ....

9. Remarks on the course of the interview

   ....

Questionnaire for judges

1. How long have you been in charge of divorce cases?

   ....

2. How many divorce cases have you conducted?

   ....

3. How many conciliatory sessions have you conducted?

   ....

4. Are the parties always able to obtain a divorce, even in want of complete and permanent breakdown of marriage[7] if they unanimously deceive the court?

   yes no

5. In your opinion, what is the mean proportion of final divorce decrees pronounced without complete and permanent breakdown of marriage?

   ....

6. What do you say to the parties at the conciliatory session?

   ....

[7] Here I explained to the interviewee the meaning in which I used the expression "complete and permanent breakdown of marriage" (See on this pp. 25-26, *supra).*

7. Did repeated conciliatory sessions occur in your practice?
   yes no (if yes) how many times? ....

8. How many of the divorce suits conducted by you resulted in reconciliation?

   ....

   Was it mainly due to:
   1°– the activity of the court?
   2°– the fact that sometimes neither party really wants divorce?
   3°– what other reasons?

   ....

9. In your opinion, should the conciliatory session be:
   Maintained in its present form?
   Modified? (if yes) What changes would you introduce? ....
   Rejected?
   Why?

   ....

10. In the course of the suit the parties contesting guilt frequently reach an agreement as to divorce without deciding the question of guilt. Is that agreement due to:
    a. the persuasion of the court?
    b. the persuasion of the barrister (or barristers of both parties)?
    c. the influence of other factors, and if so, what factors?

    ....

    Which is the most frequent: a., b. or c.?

11. How frequently do you induce the parties who do not want to become reconciled to give up contesting the question of guilt?

    ....

    Do you: usually succeed in this?
    usually not succeed in this?
    Does this persuasion take place:
    mostly at the conciliatory session?
    mostly in the further course of the suit?

12. Did you come across cases where the marriage could have been saved before the filing of the petition, but the suit aggravated the

relations between the spouses to such a degree that the chance disappeared? yes no

(If yes) How many times?

....

13. In your opinion, could the embittering influence of the suit be avoided, and if so, in what way?

....

14. In your opinion, does the rule denying the solely guilty spouse the right to claim divorce prevent husband and wife failing in their duties to each other? yes no don't know

15. Have you come across cases where the innocent defendant's consent to divorce (to divorce without deciding the question of guilt or to divorce with imputing guilt to the plaintiff) was:

the result of threat?

yes no

the result of payment?

yes no

How many cases of threat came out in your practice?

....

How many cases of payment?

....

What was the nature of the threats?

....

What was the nature of the payments?

....

In your opinion, what is the mean proportion of consents given as an outcome of: threats? ....

payments? ....

16. For what reasons do the innocent defendants refuse to consent to divorce?

a. in order to save the marriage?
b. because of the children's welfare?
c. because of malice?
d. because of hatred and revenge?
e. because of religious beliefs?
f. for other reasons, and if so, what reasons?

....

Which of those motives are the most frequent and intense?
1°
2°
3°

17. Would you be inclined to advise the legislature:
To make divorce easier?
(If yes) In what way?

....

Would you, in particular, advocate divorce of childless marriages by consent pure and simple?
yes no

To make divorce more difficult?
(if yes) in what way?

....

would you, in particular, advocate limiting of divorce to a few serious matrimonial offences, like adultery or cruelty?
yes no

To reject divorce?
To retain the provisions in force without change?
Why?

....

18. Have you any further comments on the divorce suit or other problems which we have been talking about?

....

19. Remarks on the respondent

....

20. Remarks on the course of the interview

....

Questionnaire for barristers

1. What in your opinion is the value of the conciliatory session?

....

2. In how many conciliatory sessions have you taken part since mid 1958 (in the county court)?

....

3. In how many divorce suits have you taken part since then?

   ....

4. In how many of the cases in which you appeared was the conciliatory activity of the court effective (resulted in reconciliation)?

   ....

   Were those effects due mainly:
   to the activity of the court?
   to the fact that sometimes neither party really wants divorce?
   to what other reasons?

   ....

5. Do you know any judge (or judges) who has a particularly effective way of reconciling the parties?

   yes no

   (if yes) What is the difference between his behaviour and that of other judges?

   ....

6. In your opinion, should the conciliatory session be:
   Maintained in its present form?
   Modified? (if yes) What changes would you introduce? ....
   Rejected?
   Why?

   ....

7. In how many of the cases of reconciliation mentioned above (in point 4) do you know what were the further relations between those reconciled?

   ....

   In particular: how many reconciliations resulted in working marriages?

   ....

   how many – in unhappy marriages?

   ....

   how many – in a new petition for divorce?

   ....

   how many – in an eventual divorce decree?

   ....

8. In how many cases was the divorce suit in which you appeared tried a second time, after previous reconciliation?

   ....

9. Did you come across cases where the marriage could have been saved before the filing of the petition, but the suit aggravated the relations between the spouses to such a degree that the chance disappeared?

   yes no

   (if yes) How many times?

   ....

10. In your opinion, could the embittering influence of the suit be avoided, and if so, in what way?

    ....

11. Are the parties always able to obtain a divorce, even in want of complete and permanent breakdown of marriage [8] if they unanimously deceive the court?

    yes no

12. In your opinion, what is the mean proportion of final divorce decrees pronounced without complete and permanent breakdown of marriage?

    ....

13. In the course of the suit the parties contesting guilt frequently reach an agreement as to divorce without deciding the question of guilt. Is that agreement due to:
    a. the persuasion of the court?
    b. the persuasion of the barrister (or barristers of both parties)?
    c. the influence of other factors, and if so, what factors?

       ....

    Which is the most frequent: a., b. or c.?

[8] Here I explained to the interviewee the meaning in which I used the expression "complete and permanent breakdown of marriage" (See on this pp. 25-26, *supra*).

14. Do those judges who induce the parties to give up contesting the question of guilt do it mainly: at the conciliatory session?
in the further course of the suit?

15. In what proportion of uncontested cases [9] do the parties not try to hide the causes and symptoms of breakdown from the court?
....
Why do they not hide them when the case is uncontested?
....

16. In what proportion of uncontested cases are the main causes and symptoms of breakdown hidden?
....

17. In your opinion, does the rule denying the solely guilty spouse the right to claim divorce prevent husband and wife failing in their duties to each other?
yes no don't know

18. Have you come across cases where the innocent defendant's consent to divorce (to divorce without deciding the question of guilt or to divorce with imputing guilt to the plaintiff) was:
a result of threat?
yes no
a result of payment?
yes no
How many cases of threat came out in your practice?
....
How many cases of payment?
....
What was the nature of the threats?
....
What was the nature of the payments?
....

In your opinion, what is the mean proportion of consents given as an outcome of: threats? ....
payments? ....

[9] Here I explained to the interviewee the meaning in which I used the expression "uncontested cases" (See on this pp. 43-44, *supra).*

19. For what reasons do the innocent defendants refuse to consent to divorce?
    a. in order to save the marriage?
    b. because of the children's welfare?
    c. because of malice?
    d. because of hatred and revenge?
    e. because of religious beliefs?
    for other reasons, and if so, what reasons?

    ....

    Which of those motives are the most frequent and intense?
    1°
    2°
    3°

20. Do you think that a party in a divorce suit
    always informs
    usually informs
    only sometime informs
    his barrister about the main circumstances indicating the degree and permanency of marital failure?

21. Have you any further comments on the divorce suit or other problems which we have been talking about?

    ....

22. Remarks on the respondent

    ....

23. Remarks on the course of the interview

    ....